HOME RUN
PREACHING SERMONS THAT CONNECT
2013 Edition

W. Kirk Brothers

INTRODUCTION

I PERIODICALLY DO the play-by-play of Freed-Hardeman University baseball games on FM91 radio station in Henderson, Tennessee. One of the things I enjoyed most is announcing a home run. "It could be, it might be, it is! Ding-dong that pitch is dead. Homerun Lions!" Home runs are fun. The fans come to their feet. Teammates meet the batter at home plate and engulf him in a mob of high fives and shouts. What a blast!

Hitting a ball over the fence yourself is even more enjoyable than watching someone else do it. I had hit "in-the-park" home runs during softball games on various occasions but I had never hit one over the fence. It finally happened for me at the "world renown" camper versus counselor softball game during Horizons Leadership Training Camp at Freed Hardeman University. We were playing on the woman's softball field. The fence was only 200 feet away. I knew it was my chance to "park one" in a live game. In my first at-bat, with two runners on base, I sailed one over the centerfield fence. The counselors lined up on the third base line to welcome me home. It was my moment in time. What a blast!

As much as I have enjoyed these home-runs, there is something I enjoy much more. It is a young mother who walks up to me after a mother's day sermon and says, "Thanks for that sermon, it is just what I needed." It is the person who responds to the invitation and says, "Your sermon made me realize that I needed to come back to God." It is the person who walks down the aisle and says, "I want to be baptized into Christ." I can potentially have the joy, each time I preach, of watching a person in the audience come out of sin. God can work through me to hit a Home-run (God is the power). What a blast!

As preachers, we must strive to preach lessons that "connect" with people's lives. Our mission is to connect heaven with earth, 1st century with the 21st century. Our goal is to draw people "home" to the Father. That is the most wonderful, thrilling, exciting, terrifying, and humbling opportunity in the world. God had but one son and He was a preacher. There is no more important thing we can do with our lives than preach the Gospel. Let's learn to do it the best way we can. This workbook is designed to help you learn how. This book is especially aimed at "rookies" just learning to preach, but it will be helpful to "seasoned veterans" as well. I learned all of it from someone else. Maybe the "coaching tips" I received from others will help you hit a "home run." Swing for the fences!

This workbook will be divided into four sections: ROUNDING THE BASES, BATTING PRACTICE, THE BULLPEN and THE PRESS BOX.

Note to Teachers: Former Freed-Hardeman president, H. A. Dixon, had underlined the following in his copy of John Broadus' monumental work, Preparation and Delivery of Sermons: "To interpret and apply his text in accordance with its real meaning, is one of the preacher's most sacred duties" (32). This should remind us that we are not just training boys how to speak, we are training them to accurately interpret, apply, and explain God's Word so others can believe it and live it out in our lives. We are doing Godwork. Let us do it well.

SECTION ONE
ROUNDING THE BASES

THE MAKING OF A SERMON

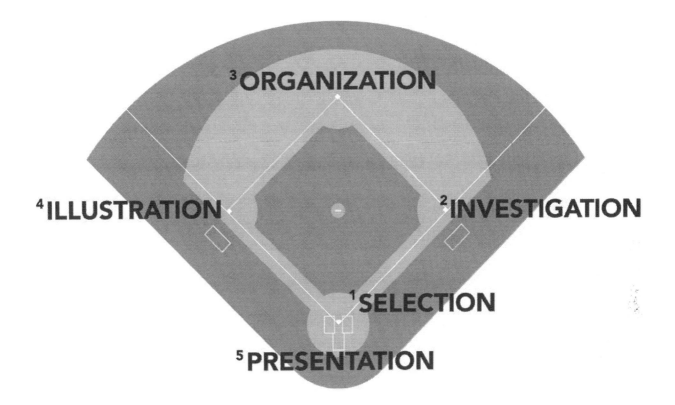

Stepping to the Plate: Selection - You must select the topic, text, character, etc. that you are going to focus on.

First Base: Investigation - This is the part of the process where you study to see what the Bible is trying to say in the text you are focusing on or about the topic you are considering.

Second Base: Organization - This is the stage in which you organize all the information you have gathered while studying into a logical form that allows you to remember it and present it to the audience in such a way that they can remember it. You also have to eliminate unnecessary information during this stage.

Third Base: Illustration - At this point in the process you apply what you have learned from studying the Bible to your audience. You add illustrations that make the message understandable, motivates the audience to take action, and helps them to remember your message. You also add the introduction and conclusion to your talk at this point.

Home Plate: Presentation - This is the point at which you actually deliver your sermon or devotional to the audience. You want deliver it in such a way that they can understand what God wants them to do, can remember the message, and can apply it to their lives after the presentation is completed.

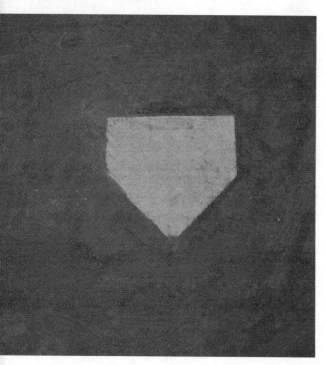

CHAPTER ONE

STEPPING TO THE PLATE

Selection: Picking the Topic

Several things must be considered and decided before a batter can get a hit. These include the batters place in the batting order, the bat he is going to use, his ability to focus, his stance, and his choice of pitches to swing at. There are also several things that must be considered before a preacher can put together a successful sermon. This section deals primarily with the choice of a passage or topic. Some say that half the work of preaching is done once a topic or text has been chosen. I try to stay three months ahead in laying out my sermon plan. This allows my elders to know what is coming and gives me plenty of time to prepare.

THE BATTING ORDER: THE PURPOSE OF THE GATHERING

Before the game, a baseball coach may tape the batting order to the wall of the dugout. Each player will look to see if he or she is in the lineup and where he is in the batting order. How a person bats will be affected by where he is in the order. For example, a leadoff hitter will probably take a pitch on a three-ball count while a cleanup hitter may swing away. This is because the goal of the leadoff hitter is to get on base and the goal of the cleanup batter is to drive in runs. Likewise, the setting we find ourselves in will often influence the topic or text we choose for a sermon. Consider the following:

A.   How long is the lesson to be? (5 min, 10 min, 30 min, etc.)
B.   Is it to be a Sunday morning or a Wednesday night lesson?
C.   Is it to be a lesson for a banquet, retreat, youth rally, etc.?

CHOOSING YOUR LUMBER: WHAT CAN YOU HANDLE?

I toured the Louisville Slugger Plant in Louisville, Kentucky a few years ago. It was interesting to see how the bats were made and to see the different types. Many professional players pick up a bat before stepping to the plate that has been tailor-made for them. My cousin is a relief pitcher for the Rockies and he has a bat with his name on it. My cousin's bat would be tough for a little league player to handle. Players need to use equipment appropriate to their level of experience. Likewise, preachers should choose a topic they can handle. Consider the following:

A.   Your experience: There are some topics we may not have enough knowledge or experience to handle (Holy Spirit, head coverings, etc.).

B.   Your interest: When first learning to preach, it is best to speak on things you enjoy studying, talking about, or have experience with (love, faith, honesty etc.).

STEROIDS: ARE WE USING AN ILLEGAL POWER SOURCE?

PREPARE WITH PRAYER: The phrase, "The Steroids Era," has now become a part of professional baseball. Many of the stars in recent years have been linked to steroid use (Bonds, McGwire, A-Rod, etc.). The crowds cheered them for a while but now their records are tainted because they cheated. There may be preachers who are guilty of doing the same thing spiritually. We may be cheating by using someone else's sermons and not giving them credit. Even worse, we may be preaching by our own ability and not relying on and seeking God's power to help us. We should never stand before God's people until we have knelt to pray before their God (1 Tim. 2:8; 2 Thess. 3:1).

TAKING YOUR STANCE: ARE WE PREACHING THE WORD OR THE WORLD?

I enjoy watching ESPN. Often commentators and analysts will analyze a batter who is hitting well or one who is in a slump. They will frequently notice his stance in the batters box and how it may have changed. It is interesting to note how a batter's stance can affect his success at the plate. Likewise, we must stand firmly on the Word of God if we want our preaching to be successful (Ps. 119:133). We

WE CANNOT SPEAK HIS WORD IF WE DO NOT KNOW IT.

must not have sermons built on opinion or illustrations. We must stand on the Word and not the world. If we are not going to preach the Word, we need to stay in the dugout!

A.   What makes a great sermon? Organization? Smooth delivery? Enthusiasm? No! It is only great if it is filled with the word of God (2 Tim. 3:16-17).

B.   We only have the authority to speak if we speak God's words.

C.   The preacher must "interpret, apply and illustrate, but . . . he must not invent.... preaching...is letting God speak out of his Word" (Broadus 19).

     D.   We cannot speak his Word if we do not know it.

PICKING PITCHES: WHO IS YOUR AUDIENCE?

Each pitcher has a number of pitches he can use. He is better with some than others. It is important for a batter to know a pitcher's strengths and weaknesses. When at the plate, he must often consider which pitch the pitcher is going to throw. When a ball is coming toward you at 90-plus miles per hour, it is often helpful to think ahead. If you are prepared for a fastball and the pitcher throws a change-up, then you will probably swing ahead of the pitch. You need to adjust your swing to the pitch that is being thrown in order to be successful. It is the same in preaching. Just as the batter's swing must meet the pitch thrown to him, our message must meet the needs of the audience we face.

A.   Who are we speaking to and what are their needs? (Youth, senior saints, etc.)

B.   What are the current issues in the community/country? (abortion, liquor, etc.)

C.   What are the relevant current events in the news? (bombing, tornado, etc.)

D.   What are the needs and current events within the congregation? (gossip problems, appointing elders, etc.; I pass out a survey to the congregation periodically to get their input on needs and topics)

E.   Are there issues/topics that the elders would like addressed from the pulpit?

F.   Possible Sermon Topics (cf. Holland, Sermon 42-45).

     1.   Sermons on basics (belief in God, baptism, the Church, the Bible).

     2.   Sermons on Christian responsibilities (worship, giving, evangelism).

     3.   Sermons on Christian living (worry, peace, purity).

     4.   Sermons on Current issues (abortion, gambling).

     5.   Sermons on last things (heaven, hell, judgment).

     6.   Preach through entire books of the Bible. This is the most effective way to cover all the needed topics.

CONCLUSION

"Preaching is the communication of truth by man to men" (Phillips Brooks 5). John Stott describes the goal of preaching as "bridging the gap between two worlds" (139). Our goal is to connect the 1st century with the 21st century. If this communication and connecting is going to take place, we must consider carefully the five elements we have just studied in "stepping to the plate."

CHAPTER TWO
THE SINGLE

Preparation

Guy N. Woods states that learning is not just reading or just being able to understand what you read. Learning is being able to explain what you have studied to others (11-12). We should strive to know the word such that we can share it. The importance of knowing the Word is stressed in Hebrews 4:12-14. We want to be able to handle the "mature" portions of the Word. Hebrews 4 teaches us that to do so we must "because of practice" have our "senses trained to discern good and evil" (4:14). Coaches give players tips that will help them on the field. This section contains some "coaching tips" on Bible study that can help you as you train in the Word of God. We will focus on SIGNALS, SETTING, SEEKING, and STUDY.

SIGNALS

A.   It is important in baseball for players to pay attention to their coaches when batting or running the bases. The coach will give a player signals telling him when to bunt, hit and run, steal a base, or stretch a single into a double.

B.   In studying God's word there are certain "coaching guidelines" we must adhere to in order to understand the "signals" God is sending us through his Word. These guidelines are called "hermeneutics."

C.   Hermeneutics is defined as "the art and science of Biblical interpretation" (Holland, Encouraging 107).

D.   Guidelines on how God guides us (cf. North, "Hermeneutics" 26-27).

1. Direct Command: To make application of a command we must determine its level of specificity. For example, My dad was my coach in little league. Let's imagine that before one of our games my mother sent me into the store to buy drinks for the team. She would not say, "Just buy some things" (because she knew I might come back with baseball cards). Mom would be more specific and tell me to buy soft drinks. If this was all she said, then I could choose what brand, what flavor, what size, or how many. She might be even more specific and say, "Get a 2-liter Sprite that is on sale for 99 cents." The degree to which she specified what she wanted told me how much freedom I had to choose for myself. I could not choose above what was specified but I had the freedom to choose below it. Above the level of specificity, silence forbids, but below it, silence allows.

For example, Paul commands us to sing (Ephesians 5:19). We do not use instruments in worship because God did not authorize their use. We do not go above His specifics. Yet, we do have freedoms below it. We can use books or sing from memory. We can sing parts or in unison.

2. Approved Example: The Bible does not command us to have elders. Yet, we have Paul's example of appointing elders in every church (Acts 14:23) and the qualifications of elders which he gave in 1 Timothy 3 and Titus 1. Thus, we rightly conclude that churches should have elders. We also have examples of people doing bad things in the Bible (cf. Saul, Samson, etc.). That is why we say we follow examples that are approved by God in Scripture, not examples he disapproves of.

3. Inference: 1 Timothy 3:2 reveals that elders are to be "the husband of one wife." We correctly infer from this that women are not to be elders.

4. Consider custom: We must take ancient customs into consideration in conjunction with the guidelines above (cf. 1Thes. 5:26 with Luke 22:48). Yet, do not overdo this!

SETTING

The Key Principle of Bible Study is to study the verse in its *context*.

"Context" refers to the setting that a verse is found in. Imagine that a pitcher for the Chicago Cubs is pitching to a batter who plays for the Atlanta Braves. The batter hits a line drive that strikes the pitcher on the side of the head and knocks him to the ground. A team trainer rushes to him and begins asking him questions: "Do you know who you are?," "Do you know where you are?," and "How many fingers am I holding up?" If pitcher does not answer these questions properly then he is going to be removed from the game and taken to the hospital. If he is confused and doesn't know where he is, he is probably not going to make wise pitching decisions. He becomes a danger to himself and others.

Likewise, if we use a verse and do not understand the setting it is in, we become dangerous to others and ourselves. We will make unwise applications of the passage. We must ask questions like: "Who is speaking?," "Where is he?," "To whom he speaking?," "Why does he say what he says?," "What problem is he dealing with?," and "What is happening when he says it?" Answering these questions will help us to understand what a verse means. For example: Our response to the statement, "Bow down and worship me," will differ greatly depending on whether we learn that it is spoken by God or by Satan. Let's make sure we understand the setting of a verse before we state what it means.

SEEKING TRUTH: SECRETS TO SUCCESS IN SEEKING TRUTH.

Some say, "You can prove anything with the Bible." In reality, if you follow the following steps below, you can only prove what God said. The memory device we will use is the song, "Take Me Out to the Ball game," by Jack Norworth. When exegeting a passage ("drawing out" God's meaning), we want to avoid the "seventh inning stretch." We do not want "stretch" the truth of a passage to fit our purposes. We want to avoid putting our thoughts into the verse of Scripture.

SONG	SIGNIFICANCE
Take me out to the ball game, Take me out with the crowd. Buy me some peanuts and cracker jack, I don't care if I never get back, Let me root, root, root for the home team, If they don't win it's a shame. For it's one, two, three strikes, you're out, At the old ball game." (Jack Norworth)	Take out Bible and read passage (3 versions) Learn about crowd: author, audience, book What customs relate to text? Go back to history of passage (kings, events) "Root" for the meaning of key words It's a shame not to note immediate context Check "out" what three other writers say GAME: Give Author's Meaning Expression - Write the main point/s of the passage

"Take me out": Take out your Bible and read the text. Many go straight to commentaries when preparing their lessons. The use of commentaries should come late in the sermon preparation process. I recommend reading the verses in three different reliable translations.

"With the Crowd": Learn about the audience of the text ("the crowd").

> 1. Who wrote the book? Where from? To whom did he write it? When was the book written? What is the central idea of the book?
> 2. Compare O.T. and N.T. introduction books, commentary introductions, Bible handbooks, and some study Bibles.
> 3. The literary context of the passage very important. My friend, Doug Burleson, likes to try to read through the entire book that contains the passage being explored so that he can get a feel for the literary context.

"Peanuts/Cracker Jack": These are customs, food we buy at baseball games. Passages of Scripture have "customs" associated with them as well.

> 1. What customs affect the verse? (Habits, weights/measures, money)
> 2. What type of literature is it? (a story, parable, proverb, letter, etc.)
> 3. Compare commentaries, Bible encyclopedias, and customs books.

"Ever get back": We need to go "back" and learn the historical information connected to the passage.

> 1. What city were the characters in? What was it like?
> 2. Where does this story fit in history? (dates, events, kings, etc)
> 3. What do you know about the characters? (history books, Bible)
> 4. Compare commentaries, Bible encyclopedias, and customs books.

"Root, Root": "Root" for the meaning of Key words.

> 1. Learn all the Greek and Hebrew you can. It will be a tremendous asset is studying God's Word. Be very careful in how you use these original languages in a sermon. Don't claim or use expertise you do not have.
>
> 2. Define any words that you do not understand and words that are central to the thought of the verse.
>
> 3. Make sure you know the meaning of the English words first (Webster's Dictionary) and then define it in Greek or Hebrew.

4. Here are some key questions and considerations as you study:

- Are there any words you don't understand or that your audience might not understand? (cf. "propitiation").
- Are there any words that are "theme words" in the book? (cf. "joy" Philippians).
- Look for verbs and participles (cf. the list of participles in Eph. 5:19-21).
- Look for the tense of verbs (cf. Rom 5:1-21 and the interaction between past, present, and future tenses).
- Look for "petition verbs" (I beseech, urge, etc.) & words that follow them in the text (cf. Romans 12:1, 15:30).
- Look at key theological words (grace, mercy, etc.).
- Define the terms in light of their usage in this passage.

5. Can use a word-study book (Mounce's Expository Dictionary, Kittel's Theological Dictionary, Robertson's Word Pictures), a Lexicon (Bauer, Thayer, etc.), and translation comparison in this process.

6. Most words will have more than one meaning listed in the lexicon. Do not combine all the definitions you find or just pick a meaning that you like. Most words have only one meaning in the sentence and setting they are in.

7. Look at how the terms are used in the sentence and the sentence structure itself. For example, is it a verb, noun, preposition, or subject of the sentence? The context of the verse and how the word is used in the sentence will guide you toward the appropriate meaning.

8. Do not just break down a Greek word to find the meaning. Many Greek words are a combination of words (like the word ekklesia). Analyzing the words separately does not necessarily tell you what they mean together. Imagine if a person studying English tried to figure out what the word "butterfly" means by breaking it down into the terms "butter" and "fly" (is not butter that flies).

9. Reinecker's Linguistic Key to the New Testament can be helpful in learning the tense and mood of the original Greek. Many computer programs have features that assist in doing word studies. The Accordance software for MAC, for example, will parse every word in the New Testament. There are many things

that might be learned from this process. For example, you might explore the term charis, translated as "grace" and used 155 times in the New Testament. You will notice that the term generally referred to an unforced favor or kindness done for someone else. Additional study will reveal that God added to the meaning of the term. He used is of kindness shown to not only to those who did not deserve it but also to those who actually deserved the opposite. You might also note linguistic features like the series of participles in Ephesians 5:15-20 that give evidence that a person is "filled with the Spirit" or consider the present tense verbs that are critical in the interpretation of 1 John 1.

"It's a shame": It is a shame not to look at the immediate context/setting.
1. Look at the paragraph your text is in and the one before and after it.

2. Find where the discussion/events begin of which the verse you are studying is a part. You may need to backtrack several paragraphs or chapters.

3. Look at the key characters and the events of the discussion in which your passage is a part.

"Three strikes you're out": Check "out" input of 3 authors/scholars.

1. Bible writers: How does it fit the Bible's message (salvation in Christ)? What do other Bible references say? Note how the words and phrases in your text are used elsewhere in the Bible. You can use a concordance or The Treasury of Scriptural Knowledge.
2. Other writers: Compare commentaries, articles, sermons, etc.
(Save till last/compare at least three).

G.A.M.E.: Give **A**uthor's **M**eaning **E**xpression: Write (express) the main point/s or theme/s of the passage (what Haddon Robinson called the "big idea").

SWINGING: MAKING CONTACT WITH THE WORD

It is a great feeling to swing the bat and make good contact with the ball. Instead of a slow grounder or a weak fly ball, a line drive sails over the infielders' heads. It is an even greater feeling to make contact with the Word of God. We must seek to understand the inspired writer's message and then organize, illustrate, and apply that message such that it connects with the audience. It is easier to put a puzzle together if you see a picture first and then you are handed one piece at a time (Kougl 43). We must decide what the picture is that God is painting in his Word and present it to the audience. We must also decide the order in which to present the pieces (main points). When putting a puzzle together you start with the outside pieces and then add the rest. Similarly, in sermon preparation, we work from the general down to the specifics.

PREPARING TOPICAL SERMONS

This is a sermon in which the text supplies only the subject of the sermon. Some subjects or issues need to be viewed from a larger perspective than just one verse or set of verses. I call these sermons "Blimp's eye view" sermons. It is looking at a subject from the overall biblical perspective like a blimp gives the audience and overall view of a football field during a game.

WHAT TO SAY
Subject and text

Memory glue: T

TOPIC: Refer to chapter one on how to choose the topic.

>   1. Consider the occasion, the age of the audience, the audience's needs, etc. "In a sermon of this type, the subject is usually the genesis of the discussion and the text is of secondary consideration" (Guild 73). This does not mean the text is of secondary importance, it just means that the process starts with the subject instead of a text.

>   2. Do not just jack up a passage and run a sermon under it. In other words do not write a sermon saying what you want to say and then go and try to find a group of verses that you can stick with it. Let the Bible tell you what to say. "We are not speculators, but expositors" (Stott 213). Our job is not to speculate on what we think, but to "draw out" the message God wants to teach and apply it to people's lives.

TEXT: Once the subject has been chosen, pick an appropriate text/s or group of passages to build the sermon on (you may do this in the opposite order - you may from a text decide on the subject). Memory glue: PICK

>   1. **P**ASSAGES: Use your Concordance and/or Topical Bible to find passages that deal with your subject.

2. **I**NVENTORY: List the most relevant passages. Identify the passages that reveal the aspects of your topic that you want the audience to learn. Time will often prevent you from discussing every verse. Note the passages that reveal the key elements of your topic or that reveal information about the topic that is most relevant to the congregation or group you are speaking to. Consider your audience. If they are teenagers then you might choose the verses related to your topic that will be the most helpful to teenagers.

3. **C**OMMENT: Jot a brief summary of each verse beside each verse in your notes.

4. **K**EY: From these texts choose one key text that best reveals your subject and the message your audience needs. You will use other passages in your lesson but this is the text you will stress. It is the passage that can be put in the bulletin or can be read aloud before the sermon. The audience will probably not remember all the verses you give them. Yet, they are more likely to remember one. So pick a key verse that summarizes well your message.

WHAT IT SAID
Find the message of the inspired writers.

Memory glue: MESSAGE

1. **M**EANING: Define unknown and key words in your relevant passages and especially in your key text (words like "atonement," "propitiation," etc.; cf. books such as Mounce's Expository Dict.). Note how these words are used in the passage (noun, verb, etc.).

2. **E**XPLORE ELSEWHERE: Note how the key words are used elsewhere in the N.T. (words like "faith," "forgiveness," etc.) and jot a brief summary (use a concordance to find these words).

3. **S**ETTING: Learn the setting of the verse.

A. *Whole: Book context.* Who wrote it? When did he write it? To whom did he write it? Why did he write it? What type of literature is it? (cf. O.T. and N.T. introduction books).

B. *Where: Historical context.* Where does this fit in history? Are there key leaders or customs that affect the text? (cf. commentaries/customs books).

C. *Wrap: Immediate context.* Note the discussion that "wraps" around the verse you are considering. Look at the verses before and after the verses you are studying: Who is speaking? To whom is he speaking? What event is taking place? What type of literature is it? (cf. commentaries for type of literature). Note where the discussion starts that leads up to your verse.

4. **S**UBJECT MATTER: Now write down the main point of your text/s and a theme for your lesson. I call this theme the "Biblical Bull's Eye." I stress it at the beginning and end of my lessons.

5. **A**PPLY AGAIN: Define key words and learn the settings for the parallel passages that you jotted down in your concordance and topical bible searches. You do not have to do this for every verse you found in your search, only those that you think will be most helpful with your lesson. Add your findings to your notes.

6. **G**IST: Write down the main point of each of these passages. Many of these verses will become the "parallel passages" which support your main points.

7. **E**XAMINE: Examine what other competent scholars have to say on any of these passages and add them to your notes (use commentaries, sermons, articles, etc.).

- Remember that these scholars are not inspired. They are only men.
- Listen to more than one man's opinion (I recommend at least three).

WHAT IT SAYS
to modern world

Memory glue: WORLD

1. **W**RITE: Look through the list of passages from your concordance search for 2-5 main points on your subject and write them down. Suppose your sermon is on faith. One verse may stress that faith is to be in God (Heb. 11:6). Another

verse may stress that faith focuses on the unseen (2 Cor. 5:7). There may be a third that stresses that the Word of God helps us to have faith (Rom. 10:17). These three ideas (and passages) could become three main points for your lesson. It is important that these points tie into and support the theme/thesis for your lesson (the biblical bull's eye).

2. **O**RGANIZE: Organize your parallel passages and any relevant comments under the appropriate main point (these items become the supporting material for your main points).

3. **R**ELEVANT: Reread the verses and note how they relate to the main point you assigned them to. Keep those that best explain and illustrate the point and eliminate the rest.

4. **L**IGHT: Add any observations and explanations that will shed light on your points and aid in understanding. For example you may observe that the work of the Holy Spirit is like that of a spotlight. He focuses his light away from himself. You might note that another word that might be used for "faith" is "trust."

5. **D**O: Think about how the points apply to your audience and write it under each point. Michael Moss notes, "The preacher or teacher must have his Bible in one hand and today's newspaper in the other. He must know his people and how they think. He must lead them to see the implications of the Word of God for their lives" (Mathis 216). It is not enough to tell people what the text means on Sunday; we must help them to see what they must do on Monday.

HOW TO SAY IT
Reaching the Audience
Memory glue: `SPAN`

1. **S**TORIES: Look for Bible examples, modern stories, poems, and other illustrations that will help the audience understand and remember your lesson and the main points. Illustrate each main point as well as the introduction and conclusion.

2. **P**REPARE: Prepare an introduction and conclusion.
   Introduction:
   - TOPIC is introduced.
   - TOW in your audience. Attract attention.
   - TELL your biblical bull's eye and main points.

Conclusion:
- • SUMMARIZE your main points.
- • SELL them on the sermon. Use illustrations to drive your point home and motivate them to action.
- • SPECIFY actions that should be taken.
- • SEEK TO SAVE. Give the plan of salvation.

3. **A**TTENTION: Word your title and main points to gain attention and aid memory (catchy phrase, same letter, rhyme, alliteration). I often use "memory glue." In the previous section on the conclusion of the sermon I used the letter "S" as my memory glue: Summarize, Sell, Specify, and Save.

4. **N**OTES: Prepare a final preaching outline.

A. Make sure it is easy to use while delivering your sermon and   make sure your notes are neat.

B. Remove all unnecessary info from your notes to make the preaching outline but leave enough info so that you can remember what you want to say.

- • Some write out a complete manuscript of their lesson. I do not do this, but there are many advantages to it (publication, re-use of the lesson in the future, etc.).
- • If you do write out a complete manuscript, do not read it from the pulpit or memorize it. Memorize ideas and concepts not every word in the manuscript.
- • Reduce your manuscript to outline form before preaching it.
- • The setting of the talk will affect what type of notes you have. If there is no podium on which to place your notes, you either need to be able to speak without notes or you might paper-clip them in your Bible. Learn the setting of your talk ahead of time. I preach all sermons from my iPad.

C. Your supporting material for each main point will be:
- • Relevant scriptures and their meaning.
- • Relevant comments by scholars.
- • Relevant definitions of key terms linguistic features of the original Greek.

- Comments, explanations or restatement of thoughts.
- Illustrations, Bible examples, statistical information, poems, etc.
- Application of the point to people's lives.

PREPARING EXPOSITORY SERMONS

This is a sermon in which the text supplies the subject, the main points, and the sub points (a "Textual" sermon only gets the subject and main points from the text). Instead of searching through other scriptures for main points, you get your main points from the text you are studying. Stafford North defines expository preaching as follows:

Expository preaching is a method for finding in a passage of scripture the fundamental message the writer desired to convey, capsuling that message so it can be easily grasped, and elaborating on that message primarily with material from the passage itself.... To prepare an expository sermon, the preacher first analyzes a passage to find a central truth the Holy Spirit put there to meet a need of his audience. He then finds several parallel thoughts from the passage that "expose" this central truth to light. Then, primarily with quotations and illustrations from the passage, from elsewhere in Scripture, and from life, the preacher shapes the message to inform and motivate the listeners. (Mathis 219-20)

Tom Holland notes that expository preaching is the
(1) Interpretation, (2) Amplification, and (3) Application of a passage of scripture (Encouraging 86). There are several advantages to such preaching (cf. Holland, Encouraging 48-56):

- It emphasizes the Word. All Scripture is God-breathed (2 Tim. 3.16-17) and is what shall judge mankind (John 12.48).
- It allows God to chose the subject. People will not think you picked out a topic just to "get at them."
- It gives you an unlimited source of material.
- It gives variety to your preaching.
- It gives us the authority to preach.

WHAT IT SAID
Intro books, commentary, word studies

1. **M**EANING: Read the verse several times. Read it in other translations/languages. Note key ("faith," "forgiveness" etc.) and unknown words ("propitiation" etc.), define their meaning, and write down the definitions (cf. word study books like Mounce's Expository Dictionary or Rienecker's Linquistic Key, and the "parsing" feature in programs like Accordance can help). Notice how the words are used in the passage (noun, verb, preposition, participle, etc.). (see "Root, root, root" section on pages 9-10)

2. **E**XPLORE: See how the key words are used in other passages (cf. a concordance or The Treasury of Scriptural knowledge).

3. **S**ETTING: Learn the setting/context of the passage (intro books, commentaries, manners and customs books, etc.).

> A. *Whole: Book context.* Who wrote it? When did he write it? To whom did he write it? Why did he write it? What type of literature is it? (cf. O.T. and N.T. introduction books).
> B. *Where: Historical context.* Where does this fit in history? Are there key rulers or customs that affect the text? (cf. commentaries/customs books).
> C. *Wrap: Immediate context.* Note the verses before and after the verses you are studying: Who is speaking? To whom is he speaking? What event is taking place? What type of literature is it? (cf. commentaries for type of literature). Note, where the discussion leading up to your verse starts.

4. **S**UBJECT MATTER: Decide on the main theme or subject matter of your passage. Write it down in a complete sentence. This becomes the "biblical bull's eye" that your sermon aims at.

5. **A**PPLY AGAIN: Note what other Bible verses say on the subject (cf. a concordance). Make sure you understand the meaning and setting of these parallel passages. You do not have to know the setting of every passage you find in your concordance search, only those you think will be most helpful with your lesson.

6. **G**IST: Write down the main point of these parallel passages.

7. **E**XAMINE: Examine what other competent scholars have to say on any of these passages and add them to your notes (give credit). (Use commentaries, sermons, articles, etc.)

- Remember that they are only men.
- Listen to more than one man's opinion (I recommend three).

WHAT IT SAYS

1. **W**RITE: Write 2 to 5 main points from the text which elaborate on the theme. Make sure they fit the theme. Don't chase rabbits! (do not discuss "side" issues that do not relate to your text). An example of drawing three key ideas/points from a passage might be using the key verbs in your verse as your main points. In Acts 26:20, for example, Paul said that his preaching called people to "repent," "turn," and "do." The Gospel should cause people to have a change in Attitude, Allegiance, and Action.

2. **O**RGANIZE: Organize the key words, definitions, the parallel passages and their meanings, as well as comments by scholars under the appropriate main point.

3. **R**ELEVANT: Note how the verses, definitions, and comments relate to the main point you assigned them to. Keep those that best explain and illustrate the point and eliminate the rest.

4. **LI**GHT: Add any observations and explanations that will shed light on your points and aid in understanding. You might comment on Acts 26:20 by observing that there must be a change in our hearts before there can be a change in our actions.

5. **DO**: Think about how the points apply to your audience and write down what the audience must do as a result of your passage. For example, you might ask your audience how Acts 26:20 fits in their lives. Do they need a change of attitude toward their sins? Maybe they are sorry for their sins, but they have never given their lives to God (faith and baptism). Maybe they are Christians, but they have not put their Christianity into action (they don't evangelize or help the needy, etc.).

HOW TO SAY IT
Concordance, illustration sources, etc.

1. **S**TORIES: Look for Bible examples, modern stories, poems, quotes, statistics and other illustrations that will help the audience understand and remember your lesson and points. Illustrate each main point as well as the introduction and conclusion.

2. **P**REPARE: Prepare an introduction and conclusion.

Introduction:
- TOPIC is introduced.
- TOW in your audience. Attract attention (illustrate).
- TELL your biblical bull's eye and main points.

Conclusion:
- SUMMARIZE your main points and how they connect to your biblical bull's eye (theme).
- SELL them on the sermon. Use an illustration to drive your point home and motivate them to act.
- SPECIFY actions to be taken.
- SEEK TO SAVE. Give the plan of salvation.

3. **A**TTENTION: Word your title and main points to gain attention and aid memory (catchy phrase, same letter, rhyme, alliteration). I often use "memory glue." In the previous section on the conclusion of the sermon I used the letter "S" as my memory glue: Summarize, Sell, Specify, and Save.

4. **N**OTES: Prepare a final preaching outline.

A. Make sure it is easy to use while delivering your sermon and make sure your notes are neat.

B. Remove all unnecessary info from your notes to make the preaching outline. Yet, leave enough info so that you can remember what you want to say.
- Some write out a complete manuscript of their lesson. I do not do this, but there are many advantages to it (publication, re-use of sermon in the future, etc.).

- If you do write out a complete manuscript, do not read it from the pulpit or memorize it.
- Reduce it to outline form before preaching it.
- The setting of the talk will effect what type of notes you have. If there is no podium on which to place your notes, you either need to be able to speak without notes or you might paper clip them inside your Bible. Learn the setting ahead of time.

C. Your supporting material for each main point will be:
- Relevant scriptures and their meaning.
- Relevant comments by scholars.
- Relevant definitions of key terms.
- Comments, explanations or restatement of thoughts.
- Illustrations, Bible examples, statistical information, etc.
- Application of the point to people's lives.

PREPARING PARABLE SERMONS

Neil Lightfoot states that parables make up over one-third of Jesus Recorded teachings (1). Jess Hall, Jr. would put the percentage at 75% and adds that parables make up 52% of the Gospel of Luke alone (Hall, "Illustrating..."). The difference in these numbers lies in what you classify as a parable. Most of the recorded parables of Jesus are found in Matthew and Luke. If you are going to explore the teaching of Jesus, you must spend time looking at his parables. The procedure for preparing sermons from parables will be very similar to that which you follow in preparing expository sermons. Yet, there are some unique features of parables which should be taken into consideration.

Herbert Lockyer notes that Parables were "a common and popular method of instruction" in Jesus day (Parables... 9). The term parable (parabole) is used 48 times in the synoptic gospels (Matt, Mark, Luke) and literally means "a throwing alongside"and "signifies a placing of two or more objects together, usually for the purpose of a comparison" (ISBE). John never uses this term. Instead, on four occasions he uses the term paroimia: "A saying out of the usual course or deviating from the usual manner of speaking, a current or trite saying, a proverb; any dark saying which shadows forth some didactic truth" (Thayer). Parables have often been described as "earthly stories with a heavenly meaning." Jesus used that which they understood to explain that which they did not understand. He used the earthly to give insight into the heavenly. In addition, Jesus used them to get attention and drive home the point he wanted to get across (like we use illustrations in our sermons).

While they brought understanding to the person who listened to them with a tender heart, they brought confusion to the person who did not listen and whose heart was corrupt (cf. Mk 4.10-12). Jack B. Scott notes that Jesus was asked why He taught in parables (Matt. 13:10). Scott summarizes Jesus' answer and the implications: "Jesus forthrightly answered that he was teaching in parables in order to reveal to his own disciples the mysteries of the kingdom of heaven while confusing others (Matt. 13:11).

From the start we learn that Jesus' parables are not given to clarify by illustration what he has been teaching. Indeed, the opposite is true. They can be understood only in the light of what Jesus taught elsewhere" (Those Puzzling Parables, p. 6). While Scott overstates and overextends his points, I think he makes some valid observations. Parables can be both confusing and enlightening. They also need to be studied in light of what Jesus teaches elsewhere. We need to teach the parables such that they are enlightening and confirming rather than confusing for our hearers.

Parables are usually found in the form of fictitious stories. Yet, these stories were true-to-life and could have happened (i.e., there are no stories about a cow jumping over the moon). These stories often included an unusual twist that surprised the audience and stressed the point (i.e., a Samaritan is held up as an example for Jews). Jesus would draw them into the story and then "wham," he dropped the "punch line" which struck the audience with the truth he was revealing. The parables were told to motivate thought and action. A response was expected.

Gordon Fee and Douglas Stuart in their book, How to Read the Bible for All its Worth, point out that there are different types of parables:

> 1. There are **TRUE PARABLES** such as The Good Samaritan (Lk 10). These are parables that have the "classic" characteristics of a parable. They are stories with a beginning, an end, and a plot.

> 2. There are **SIMILITUDES** such as The Mustard Seed (Lk. 13). These parables take normal everyday occurrences (sowing, mustard seeds etc.) and use them to illustrate a point.

> 3. There are also **METAPHORS** and **SIMILES** such as "You are the salt of the earth" (Mtt. 5.13). There are subtle differences between these and similitudes (especially in the purpose of their telling).

4. There are also **EPIGRAMS** such "Do people pick grapes from thorn bushes, or figs from thistles?" (Mtt. 7.16). These are satirical and often witty sayings which prove a point and inspire thought.

5. There are some parables that have allegorical features, such as The Wicked Tenants (Mk 12; Mt 21; Lk 20). Do not let this draw you into the trap of allegorizing every part of a parable (125).

It is important to recognize that a Parable is more like a "simile" than an "allegory." A simile is "a figure of speech comparing two unlike things that is often introduced by like or as" (Webster's 9th Collegiate, 1098). "A true allegory is a story where each element in the story means something quite foreign to the story itself" (Fee and Stuart, 127). When one allegorizes a parable, he looks for a hidden meaning in each part of the story. For example, Augustine (354-430 AD) allegorized the story of The Good Samaritan by saying that the injured man was Adam, Jerusalem stood for heaven, the thieves were the devil and his angels, the Inn is the church, the Innkeeper is the apostle Paul, etc (Lockyer, Parables... 20). Generally speaking, a parable is trying to communicate one key message or a just a few messages, and not numerous hidden ideas found in every detail of the story. The rest of the details are "window dressing" to add color to the story.

In light of this, consider the following when studying a parable.

1. Consider the circumstances of the Parable. Put special emphasis on what caused Jesus to tell the story (i.e., Matt. 18:21).

2. Take into account any customs which are relevant to the story (i.e., debtor's prisons in Matt. 18).

3. Notice any follow-up comments of explanation or application that Jesus made after telling the parable (i.e., Matt. 18:35).

4. Note the key characters and elements in the story. This is what Fee and Stuart call the "points of reference" in the story. Instead of looking for a hidden meaning in every part of the story you identify the key characters, elements, or themes in the story that tie into the central theme of the story, the setting of the story, and the conclusions that Jesus draws from it.

5. Look for the central message, truth or lesson that the speaker is trying to get across. All the other elements in the parable will be understood in light of this theme. There will be some parables that teach more than one lesson, yet, seek the central idea.

If you applied these steps to the story of The Unmerciful Servant in Matthew 18, it would break down as follows. 1) The circumstance of the parable is Peter's question in 18.21, "Lord, how often shall my brother sin against me, and I forgive him?"; 2) A key custom to consider is the amount of a denarius (one days salary for common labor) and a talent (6,000 denarii) in the first century; 3) The key follow-up comment is found in 18.35, "So My heavenly Father also will do to you if each of you, from his heart, does not forgive his brother his trespasses"; 4) The key characters or "points of reference" are the king and the unmerciful servant. Don't seek a hidden meaning for the "talents" or the "prison." Notice what the king and the servant are doing. One was merciful and the other was not. The king is merciful and punishes those who are not merciful. God functions like the king (18.35). Jesus was telling Peter to act like the king and not like the unmerciful servant; and 5) The central theme of the parable is to forgive others as God forgives you. Hopefully, this overview has now prepared you to move to the mechanics of preparing a sermon from a parable.

WHAT IT SAID   Memory Glue: MESSAGE
Intro books, commentaries, word study books

1. **M**EANING: Read the parable several times in different translations (I recommend 3). Define the key words in the parable (i.e., "forgave" in Mtt. 18:27) or words you do not understand (i.e., "talents" in Mtt. 18:24) and write down the definitions (cf. books like Mounce's Expository Dict. & Robertson's Word Pictures, as well as commentaries). You might also notice how the words are used in the parable (noun, verb etc.)

2. **E**XPLORE: See if there are accounts of this parable found in other Gospels (i.e., The Wicked Tenants found in Mk 12, Mt 21 and Lk 20). Note any differences between the accounts or ways the other accounts clarify the one you are focusing on.

3. **S**ETTING: Learn the setting/context of the passage (intro books, commentaries, manners and customs books, etc).

A. *Whole: Book context.* Who wrote it? To whom did he write it? Why did he write it? What type of literature is it? How does the parable fit into the theme of the Book? (i.e., Matthew's focus on the king and the kingdom). B. *Where: Historical context.* Where does it fit in history? Consider kings, rulers, customs etc. Are there unique customs that are involved in the parable? (i.e., first century farming habits involved in the parable of The Sower).

C. *Wrap: Immediate context.* Note the verses before and after the verses you are studying: Who is speaking? Whom is he speaking to? What event is taking place? What was happening that caused Jesus to tell the particular parable you are studying? Did someone ask him a question? (i.e., Peter's question in Matt. 18:21). To whom is Jesus speaking when he tells the parable?

4. **S**UBJECT MATTER: Decide on the central theme or point of the parable (biblical bull's eye). Write it in a complete sentence.

5. **A**PPLY AGAIN: Note what other Bible verses say on the subject (i.e., you might look up "forgiveness" in a concordance). Make sure you understand the meaning/setting of all parallel passages. You do not need to know the setting of every passage, just those you think will be the most helpful with your sermon.

6. **G**IST: Write down the main point of each of these other passages.

7. **E**XAMINE: Examine what competent scholars have to say on your passages and add them to your notes (give credit). (commentaries, articles, sermons, Lockyer's All the Parables of the Bible, etc.)

- Remember that these authors are only men.
- Listen to more than one man's opinion (I recommend three).

WHAT IT SAYS

Memory Glue: WORLD

1. **W**RITE: Write 2 to 5 main points from the text which elaborate on or focus on the main point of the parable. You may not divide a parable sermon the same way you divide a regular textual sermon:

A. You may divide the parable itself up in 2 to 5 natural divisions and discuss it accordingly (i.e., the parable of The Good Samaritan might be divided according to the men who passed by; Levite, Priest, Samaritan). The circumstances might be discussed in the introduction and the main point in the conclusion.

B. You might divide up the parable by using point one to consider the circumstances of the Parable. You might use point two to look at the details of the story and the customs and historical issues connected with it. You might use your third point to discuss the meaning of the parable, follow-up comments by Jesus, and how it applies to your audience.

C. You might divide the sermon according to lessons you learn from it. You might discuss the parable in Matthew 18 by discussing the need to forgive in point one. In point two you could discuss the fact that the world notices our actions. In point three you could emphasize that God notices our actions. The other elements of the parable can then be tied into each of these points.

D. Remember that however you divide it, you need to make sure that you consider and discuss the elements mentioned earlier: circumstances, comments of explanation and application, customs which effect the meaning of the parable, the central message, and the key characters. Also make sure you consider how to apply it to your audience.

Example: I divided the parable of The Unmerciful Servant (Mtt. 18) into four points: Seven, Story, Self and Savior. In the first point I explored Peter's question (circumstances, customs). In the second point I explored the details of the parable itself (i.e., actions of the key characters, customs; meaning of "talents" etc.). In the third point I discussed how this applies to us (i.e., comments of Jesus, central message and features such as the fact that God and our "fellow servants" notice if we don't forgive, etc.). In the fourth point I focused on Jesus as the ultimate example of forgiveness (Peter would experience this personally).

2. **O**RGANIZE: Organize all the information you have gathered to this point in your sermon preparation under the appropriate main point. These items serve as supporting material for each point.

3. **R**ELEVANT: Note how this supporting material relates to the main point to which it was assigned. Keep the supporting material which best explains & illustrates your points and eliminate the rest.

4. LIGHT: Add any observations and explanations which will shed light on your points and aid in understanding. For example, you might observe that people tend to focus more on themselves than others (from the parable in Matt. 18).

5. DO: Think about how the points apply to your audience and write down what the audience must do as a result of your passage. You might challenge the audience to call, write, or visit someone who has hurt them and make peace with them.

HOW TO SAY IT
Memory glue: **SPAN.**

1. **S**TORIES: Look for Bible examples, modern stories, poems, quotes, statistics and other illustrations that will help the audience understand and remember your lesson and points (i.e., When discussing Peter's question in Matt. 18:21, I noted that the Rabbi's said you had to forgive people seven times). Illustrate each main point as well as the introduction and conclusion (see the sample outline of Matt. 18 in the B.P. section on pages 87-88).

2. **P**REPARE: Prepare an introduction and conclusion.

     Introduction:
          • TOPIC is introduced.
          • TOW in your audience. Attract attention (illustrate). You might include a brief description of what a parable is.
          • TELL your biblical bull's eye and main points.
     Conclusion:
          • SUMMARIZE your main points and biblical bull's eye.
          • SELL them on the sermon. Illustrate to drive your point home and motivate them to action.
          • SPECIFY actions to be taken.
          • SEEK TO SAVE. Give the plan of salvation.

3. **A**TTENTION: Word your title and main points to gain attention and aid memory (catchy phrase, same letter, rhyme, alliteration). Example: I used the

letter "S" as my memory glue in my sermon form Matt. 18: Seven, Story, Self and Savior. I titled it, "The Fragrance of Christ."

4. **N**OTES: Prepare a final preaching outline.
A. Make sure it is easy to use while you are preaching.

B. Remove all unnecessary info from your notes to make the preaching outline, yet, have enough info that you can remember what you want to say.
- Some write a complete manuscript of their lesson. I do not do this, but there are many advantages to it (publication, reuse, etc.).
- If you write out your sermon, do not read it from the pulpit or memorize it (reduce it to outline form).
- The setting of the talk will affect what type of notes you have. If there is no podium on which to place your notes, you either need to be able to speak without notes or you might paper-clip them inside your Bible (keep it neat looking). Learn the setting or your talk ahead of time.

C. Your supporting material for each main point will be:
- Relevant scriptures and their meaning.
- Relevant comments by scholars.
- Relevant definitions of key terms.
- Comments, explanations & restatement of thoughts.
- Relevant customs and historical background
- Illustrations, Bible examples, statistical information, etc.
- Application of the point to people's lives.

PREPARING CHARACTER SERMONS
Seven Steps to Sermons on Bible Characters

The Bible is filled with stories about people. Herbert Lockyear states that "the Bible mentions some 3,000 men" (All the Women of the Bible, introduction). This does not include all the women mentioned in Scripture. Luke mentions 92 people by name in Acts and 62 of them are not mentioned elsewhere in the New Testament. One reason the Bible is able to stand the test of time is that God reveals his message through people. Times may change, but people are basically the same. If God used people to teach his message, then maybe we would be wise to do the same. Sermons on Bible characters make the message human and personal.

1. ACCESS scriptures on your chosen character.
   - Look up his/her name in a concordance.
   - Look up his/her name in a character study book like Lockyer's All the Men of the Bible or All the Women of the Bible.

2. ANALYZE:
   - WITNESS: Read each of the passages you found.
   - WRITE: Write down a summary of each verse.

3. ASSESS the verses you have found.
   A. OBJECTIVE: Time may not allow you to mention everything the Bible says about your character. Decide what you want to teach in the time frame you have been given. "We have the tendency to eulogize our heroes, omitting altogether their faults. But the Bible gives us a true picture: light or shade, good or evil are depicted without apology or excuse. It is a wonderful canvas of human life. Every phase of human nature is exhibited in the portraits of the Bible gallery"(Lockyer, Men... 17).

Possible approaches:
1) Overview of his/her life (consider time restraints).
2) Highlight key character traits.
3) Consider the elements (parentage, education, etc.) which may have factored into his/her success/failure.
4) Discuss defining moments in his/her life.
5) Comparison/contrast of key events in his/her life.
6) Discuss successes or mistakes he/she made.
7) Discuss key decisions he/she made.
8) Discuss privileges abused or opportunities missed.
9) Discuss opportunities he/she took advantage of.
10) Discuss key places he/she visited (Paul's journeys).
11) Discuss books he wrote.
12) Summarize lessons we can learn from him/her.
13) What can we learn about God/Christ from him/her?
14) Discuss one key event in his/her life.

   B. OUTLINE: Make a simple outline of your sermon.

C. ORGANIZE the verses about your character under your points and eliminate the unnecessary verses.

4. APPLY the "Take Me Out to the Ball Game" procedure to the verses you plan to use (cf. pages 9-10 for a fuller discussion of this).

- "Take me out": "Take out" your bible and read the passage in three different translations. Write down everything you learn.
- "With the crowd": Learn about the audience (crowd) of the text (Book author, audience, circumstances, central idea, etc.)
- "Peanuts/cracker Jack": Note relevant customs which impact the verse and what type of literature it is (story, parable letter, etc.)
- "Ever get back": Go "back" and note relevant historical info related to the passage (cities, historical events, kings, dates, etc.).
- "Root, root": "Root" out the meaning of key words.
- "It's a shame": It is a shame not to look at the immediate context (full paragraph passage is in, full discussion it is part of, paragraph before and after the passage, etc.)
- "Three strikes your out": Check "out" input from at least three other sources on the passage (Bible, commentary, sermon, etc.).
- GAME: Give Author's Meaning Expression: Write down the main point and sub-points of the passage based on your study.

5. ADD illustrations for the introduction, conclusion, and each main point.

6. AUDIENCE APPLICATION: Apply each main point to the audience and write it in your notes.

7. ADJUST for final preaching form.
- You may need to adjust points or sub-points
- You may rename your title/points to aid attention/memory.
- Make sure your notes are easy to use while preaching.
Remove all unnecessary info from your notes to make the preaching outline, yet, have enough info that you can remember what you want to say.
    - Some write a complete manuscript of their lesson. I do not do this, but there are many advantages to it.
    - If you write a manuscript, do not read it from the pulpit or memorize it (reduce it to outline form).

• The setting of the talk will affect what type of notes you have. If there is no podium on which to place your notes, you either need to be able to speak without notes or you might paper-clip them inside your Bible. Learn the setting ahead of time.

SAFE: LEGGING OUT THE HIT

Former Freed-Hardeman president, H. A. Dixon, had underlined the following in his copy of John Broadus' monumental work, Preparation and Delivery of Sermons: "To interpret and apply his text in accordance with its real meaning, is one of the preacher's most sacred duties" (32). To do this well, we must be devoted to diligent study.

A. Hindrances to study (Billy Smith, Freed-Hardeman University).
   1.   Being undisciplined.
   2.   Failing to see the importance of study.
   3.   It is hard work.
   4.   It takes time.
   5.   Messed up priorities.

B.   Habits that help: Seven Habits of Highly Effective Bible Students.
   1. Time:
      • Set up a regular time and habit of study (under strict conditions).
      • Learn to make use of small units of time (i.e., CD's in car, iPod).

   2. Tools: Build a personal Library of Bible Study aids.
      • Personal Library.
         1)   Concordance.
         2)   Bible dictionary/Encyclopedia.
         3)   O.T. and N.T. introduction books.
         4)   Commentaries.
         5)   Different translations.
         6)   Atlas.
         7)   Word study books (Greek and English).
         8)   Books on Bible times (manners and customs).

      • Other libraries: Get to know your local and church library.
      • Computer programs (PC Study Bible, Logos, Accordance, etc.) and internet libraries (Biblegateway.com, etc.; use your search engines) can be tremendous assets.
      • Study Bible: Purchase a Bible with good study aids.

1)   Look for center column references, a concordance, an introduction to each book, and a maps section.
2)   Be careful that you don't get one too big to carry.
3)   If it has commentary in it, go to the following verses and look at their comments.
   - Psalm 51:5 for their view of original sin
   - Acts 2:38 for their view of baptism
   - 1 Tim. 2:12 for their view of women's role
   - Rev. 20:6 for their view of Pre-millennialism

- There are numerous Bible apps for phones and iPads. I use Olive Tree and Glo Bible for example.

3.   Translation:
- Use a reliable and understandable translation.
- Use a committee translation as your main version.
- Don't use a paraphrase as your main version (only for comparison).

4.   Take notes:
- Take notes during sermons and classes and file your notes (apps such as Notability can be helpful).
- Make notes in the margin of your Bible. Many Bible apps allow the adding of notes and highlighting the passage.

5.   Tour:
- Go to lectureships, workshops, and meetings.
- Buy CD's/MP3s of lecture talks, download podcasts, etc.

6.   Throughout: Study systematically (through book, not hit and miss).

7.   Take in: Read, read, read! We are what we read.

CONCLUSION

Tony Gwynn of the San Diego Padres was known for the video preparation he did. He watched many hours of video of himself and the pitchers he would face. Just as each major league baseball player has certain training habits, each preacher will develop his own unique study habits. You might decide to change the order of some of the steps, but those given in this chapter will give you a basic pattern to go by. It is most important to remember to let the text say what God wants it to say, rather than making it say what we want it to! Martin Luther stated, "I study my Bible like I gather apples. First, I shake the whole tree that the ripest may fall. Then I shake each limb, and when I have shaken each limb, I shake each branch and every twig. Then I look under every leaf. I search the Bible as a whole like shaking the whole tree. Then I shake every limb-- study book after book. Then I shake every branch, giving attention to the chapters. Then I shake every twig, or a careful study of the paragraphs and sentences and words and their meanings" (qtd. in Blair). Martin sought to systematically study the text to find God's truth. We must do the same.

CHAPTER THREE

THE DOUBLE

Organization

We have arrived safely at "first base" by working hard to study the subject or text of our sermon. Yet, we have completed only a fourth of our journey. Next we must organize the information we have gathered. I helped to coach both of my daughters' t-ball teams when they were younger. When the t-ball season starts, there are always kids on the team who have never played ball before. One of the first things you must do is teach them the layout of the field. It is very common for them to run the bases starting at third base instead of first base. You have to drill them over and over on where first base, second base, third base, and home plate are. Likewise, to effectively deliver a sermon, we must understand the layout of the sermon outline.

THE SERMON SKELETON

A. **Title:** The name of the Sermon:
1. BRIEF: This makes it easier to remember.
2. RELEVANT to the message.
3. INTERESTING:
- It needs to attract attention to the Sermon.
- Examples: "You Died Last Night" or "Don't Kiss Toads."

B. **Text:** A key verse that sums up or is the basis of your message:
1. REMEMBER: This is the verse you want your audience to remember.
2. RELEVANT: It should be relevant to the topic and the audience.
3. READING: This is helpful for a pre-sermon scripture reading.

C. **Theme:** "The person who aims at nothing always hits it" (Broadus 50): I call the theme the "Biblical Bull's Eye."
1. PURPOSE: The base runner has a specific purpose when he runs. The sermon needs a purpose as well. What do we want to accomplish?
2. PUT the purpose into the form of a full sentence (word it so it is easy to remember).
3. PLACING this in your final preaching outline can help keep you focused.

D. **Introduction:** Approximately 10% of the sermon (there can be exceptions to this time limit):

1. TOPIC: It should introduce the topic and its relevance.
2. TOW: It should gain attention and cause the audience to want more. This can be done by using an illustration and explain the value of the topic.
3. TELL: It is a good idea to introduce your main points.

E. **Body:** The core of the message - Approximately 80% of the sermon:

1. SUB-DIVIDE the body into two to five main parts (less for a devotional).
    a. This makes it easier to remember.
    b. If you have more than 5 points, you need to use a   memory device.
    c. Example: Use letters in "Christian" to stand for your main points.

2. SIMPLE:
    a. Main points should be phrased in simple words, easy to remember.
    b. They can be complete sentences, a phrase, or even a single word.
    c. I often use words that begin with the same letter or rhyme. I call this "memory glue." I have used it throughout this book.
3. SUPPORT: These main divisions of the sermon will be supported by Scripture references, definitions, explanations of terms, restatement of ideas, Bible stories, illustrations, facts, statistics, and current information.
    a. Explain your point.
    b. Support your point.
    c. Illustrate your point.
    d. Apply your point.

4. SOW the sermon together with transition statements. Example: "Now that we have considered the source of sin, let us focus next on the solution for sin."

6. **Conclusion:** Approximately 10% of sermon:
    1. SUMMARIZE your main points.
    2. SELL them on the sermon. Use an illustration to drive your point home and motivate them to action.
    3. SPECIFY steps to be taken. "Our text needs to be applied as we go along. [but] . . . keep something up our sleeve [for the conclusion]" (Stott 246).

4. SEEK TO SAVE. Make sure you give the plan of salvation.

A Sample Skeleton

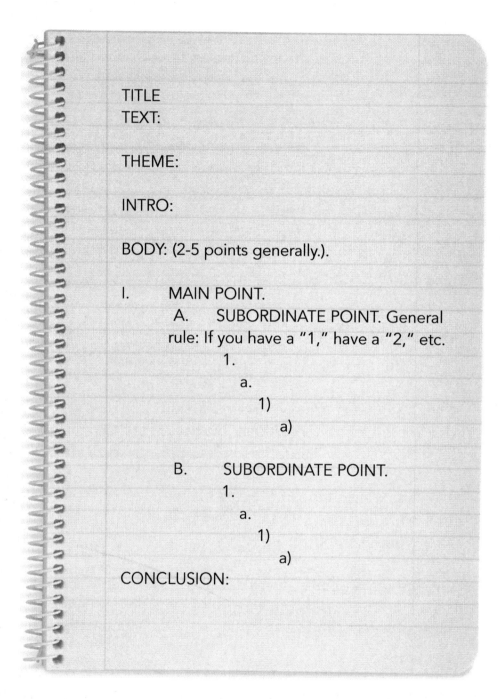

TITLE
TEXT:

THEME:

INTRO:

BODY: (2-5 points generally.).

I.   MAIN POINT.
        A.   SUBORDINATE POINT. General
        rule: If you have a "1," have a "2," etc.
              1.
                 a.
                    1)
                       a)

        B.   SUBORDINATE POINT.
              1.
                 a.
                    1)
                       a)
CONCLUSION:

TYPES OF SERMON SKELETONS / OUTLINES

TABLETOP/PROOF SERMONS

The points are like the legs of a table. As the legs hold up the table top and what is on it, so the points support or prove the theme or thesis of the lesson. The goal of the introduction is to get them interested in what is on the table. The conclusion makes them want to get a "to-go-box" to take it home with them.

MAP/PROGRESSIVE SERMONS

These are sermons in which the points advance progressively or chronologically through a topic or passage. The thesis is a destination you arrive at as you journey through the points. The goal of the introduction is to get them to read the map. The goal of the conclusion is to get them to follow it.

DRESSER/COMPARTMENT SERMONS

These are sermons in which you group the information under your points like drawers in a dresser or desk. The key is to group like things together so you know which point (i.e., drawer) contains the information you are seeking during the sermon. The introduction tells them what is in the drawers and makes them want to look. The conclusion should inspire them to "put on" the thesis.

ONE-POINT SERMONS

Andy Stanley talks about one point sermons in his book titled, *Communicating for a Change*. Andy still has multiple points (ideas and thoughts that support his central theme), he just doesn't call them points or stress them in the sermon (like saying, "Point one is....."). What he calls "one point" is basically what other preachers would call the "theme" of the lesson. All sermons have (or at least should have) a theme or thesis for the lesson. Haddon Robinson calls this the "big idea." What Stanley does is stress this "big idea" or "one point" and build his lesson around it. There is value in stressing a central thought that the audience can take home with them (many will struggle to remember multiple points). Every sermon has a central idea, we just do not always stress it. You might present a "Biblical Bull's Eye" at the beginning of the sermon. Your main points then point to that "big idea" and reinforce it. You drive that central idea or "Bull's Eye" home throughout the lesson. It is what you want them to remember when they get home. It is often wise to word the central idea or theme so that it is "catchy" and easy for people to remember (Example, "Retention Requires a Relationship").

CONCLUSION

Imagine a base runner traveling in a zigzag or meandering route around the bases. There is a good chance he will be tagged out before he completes his task. Likewise, our sermons must not meander. They need direction. We must organize the things we have learned from our study into an understandable outline and plan of attack. The outline is the skeleton on which the bones, sinew, and flesh of the sermon hang.

Attention Teachers: Hands-On Learning Activity
The "Junk Box" Sermon

A. Bring a box filled with miscellaneous junk (movies, CD's, staplers, markers, toys, books, hats, a baseball, etc.). It is good to have at least 20-30 items in the box.

B. Pour the items in the box out on the floor or a table. Tell the boys that they are going to organize a "junk box" sermon. Have the boys come forward and organize the items into similar piles. Don't tell them how to group them, let them decide.

C. Ask the students to describe their piles, what they called them, and why they grouped and named the piles the way they did. Tell them that these piles are the main points of their "junk box" sermon.

D. Ask them some probing questions:
    1. Are the piles about the same size? What can you do to balance them?
    2. Could some of the piles be combined?
    3. Are there items you could remove from some of the piles that don't really fit the pile very well?
    4. Are there too many piles? Could some of the piles be eliminated? (Try to narrow it down to 2 or 3 piles).

E. Apply this to organizing a sermon:
    1. Their piles are the main points for their "junk box" sermon and the items in the piles are the supporting material for that point.
    2. They had to organize the items in the box, eliminate certain items, and trim the piles down to a manageable size for discussion.
    3. This is basically what a preacher does in organizing his sermon. He goes through this same process with all the information he gathered while studying for his lesson.

CHAPTER FOUR

THE TRIPLE

Illustration and Finishing Touches

The triple is one of the hardest hits to accomplish in baseball. Yet, if a player can pull it off, it is also one of the most exciting. Imagine Jose Reyes (NY Mets) has an easy stand-up double, but he wants more. He decides to round second and head for third. He slides into the bag in a cloud of dust, just ahead of the throw from the outfield. Thus far, we have chosen our topic and text, we have thoroughly studied it, and we have organized it. Yet, we want more. Now we must add the finishing touches which will bring it into "third", just ahead of a mediocre sermon.

MAKING CONTACT: ILLUSTRATION

One key to getting a triple is making good contact with the ball. A seeing-eye hit which just makes it between the shortstop and third baseman will not work. The ball is going to need to find its way to a corner or bounce off a wall to be a triple. Likewise, if our sermons are going to be successful, they must make "good contact" as well. One way we help the sermon contact people's lives is through illustrations. We must not only tell them what the Word of God says, WE NEED TO MAKE IT INTERESTING!

TNT: Power of Illustrations

1. "Illustrations are to sermons what windows are to houses; they let light in upon the otherwise obscure ideas of the message" (Brown 69).

2. Illustrations bring the sermon to life.
    a. They aid in understanding, memory, proving points, getting attention, building rapport with the audience, and inspiring action.
    b. "Christianity is incarnational. Preaching should be as well. Ideas and propositions should be clothed in the flesh of illustrations" (Hall, "Where...").

3. Jesus used illustrations: Parables make up approximately 75% of Jesus recorded teaching and approximately 52% of Luke (Hall, "Illustrating...").

4. Paul used illustrations: history, the market, Olympic games, warfare, soldiers, home, marriage, school, Greek poetry, etc.

Have you ever watched an old black and white video of Babe Ruth hitting a home run? Now compare that to the brilliant color images you have seen of Josh Hamilton hitting a home run. Therein lies the difference between a sermon without illustrations and one with illustrations. It is the difference between black and white and color. Each shows the image, but one is more vibrant and life-like than the other.

TIPS on Illustrating

1. Tips from Dale Carnegie (73-80):
    a. HUMANIZE your talk.
        1) Tell stories about people (including yourself).
        2) Stories about people make your points real and personal.

    b. PERSONALIZE your talk by using names.
        1) "Imagine a story whose hero has no name" (Rudolf Flesch, qtd. in Carnegie, Effective 76).
        2) Example: Instead of saying, "A man went to his store one day," say, "George Thompson went to his store one day."

    c. SPECIFY your talk by filling it with detail.
        1) When? Where? Who? What? and Why?
        2) Example: Instead of saying, "George Thompson went to his store one day," say, "George Thompson rose in the early hours of Monday morning, July 16th, 2001 to drive to the men's clothing store which he had started 30 years before."
        3) Don't overdo this and clutter it with too much detail.

    d. DRAMATIZE your talk by using dialogue.
        1) Don't just say, "Bill and Ted argued in Ted's office."

2)   Instead say, "Bill flung open the door to Ted's office and shouted, 'How could you do this to me?' Ted responded, 'How dare you barge into my office?'"

3)   Tell them what was said. Make them part of the story.

  e.   VISUALIZE your talk by demonstrating.

    1)   Visual impressions account for 85% of our knowledge.

    2)   Use Gestures (hands, arms, face, head, etc.).

    3)   Use visuals. Don't talk about doing something, show us.

    4)   Example: Hold a golf club while telling a golfing story.

Additional Tips

  a.   METHOD:

    1)   WHEN to illustrate: introduction, conclusion, each point.

    2)   WAY to illustrate:

        a)   Vary your approach. Use different types.

        b)   Use fresh, up-to-date illustrations when possible.

        c)   Express the emotions and movements of the story:

            • Using your voice (pauses, speed variation, pitch variation, emphasis, excitement, etc.).

            • Using facial expressions (smile, frown, furrowed brow, etc.).

            • Using your eyes (widening, narrowing, etc.).

            • Using body movements (palms upward when asking a question, palms downward when calming someone, etc.).

            • Let the audience visualize the story through you. Become part of the story.

        d)   Learn the Power of Pause.

            • Pauses attract attention.

            • Pauses emphasize elements of the story.

            • Pauses show punctuation (periods, colons, etc.).

  b.   MEMORY:

    1)   REMEMBER: Learn the illustration.

        a)   Read the illustration silently.

        b)   Make a mental outline of the story. See it as a series of pictures in your mind.

        c)   Read the illustration aloud several times.

d) As you read it aloud think about words in the story the audience may not understand and incorporate their meanings into the story.

e) Make sure you have all the details correct. Tell the story in your own words. Be natural.

2) REHEARSE: Practice telling the story.
   a) Test your illustrations on friends or family members before taking them into the pulpit.
   b) Tape yourself reading or telling the story and listen.
   c) Practice in front of a mirror.

3) RIPEN: Develop your ability.
   a) Study the art of telling stories (books, classes, etc.).
   b) Practice telling stories to and reading to children.

4) RECORD: Keep a record of when, where, & how you use.

TYPES of Illustrations

1. Quotes:
   a. Someone may say something better than us, may be more of an authority, or may be more respected by the audience than we are.
   b. Make sure you quote them accurately.
   c. Either name the person you are quoting from or let it be known that the quote comes from someone else.
   d. Don't use too many. A sermon is not a term paper (Robinson 146).

2. Statistics and facts:
   a. Must be fact, not opinion.
   b. Must be authoritative (qualified source).
      1) Does he/she have experience or training in this subject?
      2) Does he/she have firsthand knowledge of this subject?
      3) Does he/she have any prejudice in this area?
      4) Does the audience respect or trust this person?
   c. Must be accurate.
   d. Must be simple (round numbers and make them understandable).
      1) Example: Say "a little over two and one half million" instead of "2,667,212."

2) Instead of saying, "The ark was three hundred cubits long," you might say, "It was a football field and a half in length."

3. Articles:
   a. Make sure the article is from a reputable source which does not have a prejudiced approach.
   b. Don't read a long article. Summarize or use short quotes.

4. Stories (See Tips earlier in the chapter):

5. Poems:
   a. Do not read it line by line, but sentence by sentence, following the punctuation marks. Avoid a sing-song or chant pattern (Loyd).
   b. Be sure to give credit for the poem.
   c. Be careful about overusing anonymous poems. It is better to use poems that are not too superficial or corny (Loyd).
   d. Make sure you can read the poem such that it reflects the poetic flow and reveals the author's intent.
   e. Define any words that the audience may not understand.

6. Songs:
   a. A song is both a poem and a story.
   b. Apply the comments above concerning poems and stories.

7. Thought provoking questions (rhetorical, "If you died today where...?"):

8. Examples from your life:
   a. Don't over do this.
   b. Don't glorify yourself.
   c. Don't hurt your family. Be very careful about family stories. Ask them before telling a story about them.

9. Visual aids: We remember more of what we see (25%) than hear (10%).
   a. SIGHT: Keep out of sight until ready to use.
   b. SEE: Make sure it is large enough to see.
   c. SECURE: Don't pass it around. Why invite competition?
   d. SHOW: Hold it up where the audience can see it.
   e. STIR: One exhibit that moves is worth more than ten that don't.
   f. STARE: Don't stare at the visual. You are talking to the audience.
   g. SIGHT: Put it out of sight when finished with it.

h.   SURPRISE: Use mystery. Cover it until used (Carnegie 155-56).

10.   PowerPoint (Microsoft Corporation) has become an effective tool in preaching. When used properly, it can be an outstanding aid. Other programs are Prezi and Keynote. SongShow Plus, MediaShout, and similar computer programs can be handy for projecting songs and scriptures.

a.   You will need the appropriate equipment (software, computer, projector, mounting equipment, etc.), lighting (not too bright), and set-up to make this work. It can be expensive.
You also need to make sure your congregation is ready for it. Don't force things on people that they are not ready for. You might try working into it gradually.

c.   Make sure the fonts are legible (Arial, Times New Roman). I try to never use anything smaller than a 24 font. I know of one expert on PowerPoint that never uses anything smaller than a 40 font. Be careful about using fancy fonts. They are often hard to see on a screen. Also remember that you may need to play your PowerPoint on a different computer. The other computer may not have all the fonts your computer has. You can prepare for this by using the standard fonts that "most" computers have: Arial, Times New Roman, Tahoma, Veranda, Symbol, Courier New, etc. If you are using a PC then you PowerPoint program will allow you to embed fonts when you choose "save as." As long as the font you used is a truetype font, it will embed the font you used into the file you saved and should stay the same on any computer. The Mac version of PowerPoint does not embed fonts.

d.   Put the presentation high on the screen so that everyone can see it whether they are sitting or standing.

e.   The color of your character font must contrast well with you background color (black/white, yellow/blue etc.). Dark backgrounds work best with light lettering (fonts) and light backgrounds work best with light colored fonts. The outlining feature on the newer versions of PowerPoint help the words to standout against the background.

f. You can vary the background color schemes, change fonts, and add graphics to increase eye appeal. You can find background pictures using Google images but you need to be very careful with copyrighted material. You can subscribe (for a fee) to PowerPoint background services like gracewaymedia.com. You can get help at sites like creationswap.com. You can also create your own backgrounds by using your digital camera to take pictures that can become backgrounds for your slides.

g. Make the presentation suitable for the age of the audience you are showing it to (i.e., young people tend to like movement and graphics while adults often like it simpler). You can purchase video clips from sites like wingclips.com. Most congregations feel uncomfortable with video clips in the auditorium but might be ok with a video clip in a class. I have only used a video clip in a sermon once or twice (use them more often in a smaller class). I decided to turn the sound down (because of the instrumental music) and just let the video play while I talked about it. Make sure you talk to your elders/leadership about this before using any video clips and make sure the clip is appropriate (don't promote movies that do evil).

h. If someone else is going to change your slides for you (and they do not have "dual screen" capability which allows them to see your current and next slide), print out a handout copy of the entire show and go over it with them (PowerPoint will allow you to print multiple slides per page, these can also be used as handouts).

i. It is also good to preview the show under the exact conditions in which it will be shown. Look at it from every corner of the auditorium and make sure it is visible (special thanks to Jeff Johnston and Jerry Elder for their input). Remember that presentations never look as good on the screen as it does on your computer. Also, test to make sure that the fonts did not adjust on the slide.

j. Do not put every single thing in your notes in the PowerPoint. If you do then you are unnecessary (they can just read your slides). I have a friend who primarily uses his PowerPoint to show pictures which cause people to think. I like to get the text in front of people and to encourage them to make notes in their Bibles. Others do not put text of Scriptures in their PowerPoints because they want people to read their own Bibles. There are the items I highlight in my PowerPoints: Title, Biblical Bull's Eye, Key Points, Biblical Text, use font color to highlight aspects of the text, & pictures/graphics.

k.   Sam Dilbeck (Corisciana, TX) frequently does sessions on preparing PowerPoint sermons at the Polishing the Pulpit workshop. For info on PTP: www.polishingthepulpit.com.

TARGETING Sources of Illustrations

1.   The Bible: The greatest source.

2.   Life: Yours and others (ask people before telling stories about them). Illustrations are all around you. Learn to look for them.

3.   Newspapers, magazines, books, etc.

4.   Movies, plays, etc.

5.   Song books, CD's, mp3's, etc.

6.   Your imagination:
   a.   It is okay to make up stories as long as you do not present them as real and as long as the truth illustrated by the story is not dependant on the story being real.
   b.   You might lead into it with a word like, "Imagine" (cf. Brown 77).

7.   Illustration books:
   a.   Okay getting started.
   b.   Don't overuse.
   c.   Often outdated.

8.   Computer programs such as Bible Illustrator (Parsons Technology).
   a.   Easy to access and organize.
   b.   Can paste into word processor.
   c.   More up-to-date than illustration books.
   d.   Can subscribe to quarterly updates which keep illustrations fresh.

e.   Can add your own illustrations.

9.   Web sites such as www.sermonillustrations.com allow search by topic.

10.   News sites: I regularly go to www.foxnews.com and peruse the current stories. I often find great illustrations in these stories.

11.   E-mail: Make sure that illustrations that come by e-mail are legitimate!

TERRORS of Illustrations: Dangers to Remember

1.   DUE: Give credit.
2.   DON'T lie. Make sure they are accurate.
3.   DIVE in (Don't say, "I am going to tell you a story").
4.   DEVELOP the point with your story. Don't tell a story just to tell a story.

STORYTELLING QUESTIONS

The following is from Mark Miller's book, Experiential Storytelling (Zondervan 2003, pp. 48-49). "Asking questions about your story is the key to unlocking creativity. It is also the tool that allows you to see your story from all sides. Here are five sets of core questions to help you understand and tell your story more effectively" (p. 48):

1.   What is the core message of the story? Is that the same message we want to convey?

2.   From whose point of view will this story come? Would the story be any stronger if told from a different point of view? Is any narration needed?

3.   What is the setting of the story? Would it be more compelling to use a new setting?

4.   What kind of conflict arises in the story? Individual vs. God? Individual vs. Satan? Individual vs. Second Individual? Individual vs. Nature? Individual vs. Society? Individual vs. Himself? Individual vs. Machine? or God vs. Satan? What are some abstract or contemporary ways we could capture this conflict?

5. What details could we add to enhance the story and what could we leave out? (pp. 48-49). "Once you know your story, know your audience, and ask the appropriate questions to broaden your perspective, you're ready to take your story to the next level–adding experience" (Miller, p. 49).

6. A few notes of caution need to be added to Miller's comments:
    a. Never change or misrepresent the facts of a true story.
    b. Never present a make-believe story as if it is real. You can use made-up stories in your lesson but you need to lead into them with a word like "imagine...."

GETTING A JUMP: THE INTRODUCTION

If a person is going to get a triple he must get out of the batters box quickly. If he delays in the box after making contact with the ball, he may not make it to third. We must also make sure that our sermons get off to a good start. Once you have thoroughly prepared the body of the sermon, put just as much effort into the introduction and conclusion.

A. TOPIC: Reveal what you plan to talk about and describe its importance.
B. TOW: They will not hear the sermon if we do not gain their attention at the start.

    1. Stories, poems, quotes, interesting statements, show of hands, promises to meet needs, and current events are all good for getting attention. I like to begin a sermon by diving right into an illustration.
    2. Build rapport with the audience. Earn the right to speak with them. You might mention people in the audience or areas of common interest. You might also mention any past contact you have had with the town you are in or the congregation you are speaking to. You might express gratitude for the opportunity to speak. I often like to get their attention with a story before I build rapport.

C. TELL: Introduce your main points.
D. TEXT: You may want to read your text. At least announce it.
E. TIME: You may also want to use the introduction to give some background for the verses you are studying (historical setting, author, etc.).

F.   THINGS to avoid.
   1.   Don't make it too long (about 10 % of sermon).
   2.   Don't begin every sermon the same way.
   3.   Don't apologize for colds, etc. It draws too much attention to the cold.
   4.   Beware of "funny stories." Are they funny? Are they offensive? Can you tell them well?

ENOUGH STEAM: THE CONCLUSION

Many a runner has gotten out of the batters box quickly only to run out of steam before reaching third. It does not matter how quickly he starts if he tires before arriving at third. Likewise, our sermons must end well if they are going to be successful.

A.   SUMMARIZE: Review your subject and main points.

B.   SPECIFY: Encourage the audience to take action. Be specific.

C.   SELL: Help them remember the sermon. Glue it to their memories.

D.   STORIES: Illustrations can help with "B" and "C" above.

E.   SHORT: Don't be too long (about 10 %). Don't preach another sermon.

F.   SAME: Don't end the same way every time. Use variety. For example, you might give the plan of salvation in the introduction instead of in the conclusion.

G.   SURPRISE: Catch them by surprise when you finish. Don't say, "In conclusion." People will pull out their songbooks and start preparing to go home. I often have them take out their song books and then I do my invitation. I want their attention when I conclude (especially for the plan of salvation). Now that many churches put their songs on a screen, the problem of people reaching for songbooks is less of a problem.

CONCLUSION

The introduction, the conclusion and the illustrations are often what make the difference between a mediocre sermon and an outstanding one. If we do not get people's attention in the beginning, they may not hear the message. If we fizzle out in our conclusion, then they may forget or ignore the message. People often remember the illustrations longer than they remember the sermon. If your illustrations accurately fit the point of your message, then you have succeeded.

Presentation

David Ortiz stepped to the plate in the 12th inning of game four of the 2004 American League Championship Series. Down three games to one to the Yankees, the Red Sox were on the verge of elimination. Ortiz hit a walk-off home run and Boston won the game. The next night he hit a game winning single in the 14th inning. The Red Sox won that series and the World Series. Some players have a talent for delivering in the clutch. Do we? Andy Stanley stresses that we are not preaching to glorify ourselves. "At some point we've got to begin caring more about the people in the audience than the person on the platform. When we do, our presentations take on real significance. Until we do, communication is really all about us" (Communicating for a Change, p. 92). John Piper says, "Preaching is the heralding of the good news by a messenger sent by God" (The Supremacy of God in Preaching, p. 31). He emphasizes that the goal of preaching is to glorify God. When we stand before a congregation to preach it is even more important than a Championship Series. What we say may influence someone's eternal destiny. We must communicate what we have prepared and practiced such that people will come home to Jesus. It is time to learn how to deliver in the clutch. Let us do our very best in our preaching so God will be glorified and the people in our audience can know Him.

THE PRACTICE FIELD: PRACTICE, PRACTICE, PRACTICE

The Atlanta Braves' first official game for the 2009 season was on April 5th against the Philadelphia Phillies. Yet, their season actually began several weeks prior to that. Their first spring training game was on Wednesday, February 25, at Lakeland, Florida against the Detroit Tigers. They put in countless hours of practice before they stepped onto the field to face the first pitch in a real game. Likewise, if we are going to be successful, we must also spend time on the practice field. We must practice our sermon delivery.

A. PREPARED sermons (Tom Holland, Sermon 18-19).
  1. The sermon is prepared when it is filled with scripture.
  2. The sermon is prepared when the scriptures are discussed and applied in light of the setting they are in.
  3. The sermon is prepared when it has been written completely, outlined, and read over until the speaker knows it well.
  4. The sermon is prepared when it has been prayed over diligently.
  5. The sermon is prepared when the preacher looks forward to preaching it.

B. POWER of practice.
  1. "Practice makes permanent." Practice builds permanent habits.
  2. "Muscles have memory." Train them to do what they should.
  3. "Proper preparation prevents poor performance" (Beatty).

C. Practice makes PERFECT (or at least perfect practice makes perfect).
  1. Memory: (cf. Carnagie, Public Speaking 79-93).

     a. SENSES: Involve as many of the senses as possible in the process of learning (cf. "Method" below).

     b. SCENES: Author Mark Twain would draw a picture representing each section of his speech. He would then throw away the piece of paper and the scenes would stay in his mind. Others paint mental images in their mind of each part of their talk. They then replay the pictures like a slide show in their mind while they are speaking.
     c. SENTENCES and STORIES. Put your main points into the form of a sentence or story. Consider the following examples.
  1. Earlier we learned how to study a passage by using the words of "Take Me Out to the Ball game."
  2. Ten Plagues: "Once upon a time there was a pond of BLOOD and some FROGS crawled out of it. The frogs had LICE and some FLIES were buzzing nearby. The flies were buzzing over a DEAD COW which had BOILS on it. HAIL was falling from the sky onto the dead cow and LOCUST were riding on the hail. This all took place in the DARK at a GRAVEYARD."

d. SAME/SIMILAR: Use words to represent each point that begin with the same letter or sound similar ("believe, befriend, bestow").

e. ASSOCIATION. Associate something you want to remember with something else (especially something you already know). Dale Carnagie uses this method to remember lists. He creates mental images for the numbers 1-20. He then creates a mental image of what he wants to remember and ties the two together.

Here are some of his picture numbers:

a) One-Run: Picture a horse running and put what you want to remember on his back.

b) Two-Zoo: Picture what you want to remember in your favorite exhibit at the Zoo (Apes, Zebras, etc).

c) Three-Tree: Place what you want to remember at the top of a tree.

For preaching. you can use this to remember your points or things you need to list during the sermon. You might use a "maestro" to remember the main story in your "intro" or "confusion" for remembering your "conclusion" story.

2. Method

a. READ over the lesson several times silently. Highlighting portions of your manuscript and outline with different colored highlighters can aid with memory (more senses involved the better). My system: scripture-green, points-yellow, sub-point-blue, illustrations-pink.

b. WRITE your title, text, theme, and main points on a piece of paper until you can do them from memory.

c. REHEARSE the lesson without your notes. Just preach what you remember. Don't go back and look at your notes while preaching. If all you are able to do is the introduction, that is okay.

d. REPEAT the Reading and Rehearsal until you are able to work all the way through the sermon without your notes. Work on memorizing your ideas, not the exact wording.

e. REFLECTION : Practice in front of a mirror (note habits, posture).

f. RESPONSE: Practice in front of a friend (ask them to critique).

g. RECORD yourself and listen (note pitch, power, pace, and pause).

h. RECOVERY: Don't practice too close to delivery (drains energy).

i. REST: Practice at least a day before you preach. Marilynn Larkin states, "Brain regions that are activated when a person learns a new task are reactivated during sleep, suggesting a relationship between sleep and memory processing, says Pierre Maquet (Institute of Neurology, University College, London, UK)."

j. Wendell Winkler always said, "Know that you know that you know" (Dan Winkler). Make sure you know what you prepared.

PRACTICE reading scriptures (see pages 93-94 and cf. McComisky).

1. PRINCIPLES:
   a. PURPOSE of scripture reading is to impress the hearers with the:
      1) Authority of Bible: Our reading will cause the audience to respect or disrespect the Word of God.
      2) Author's intent: We are the original author's means of getting his message across to the congregation.
         • Emphasis (what did the author want stressed).
         • Emotions (fear, worry, hope etc.).
   b. PROBLEMS:
      1) Reader: Our goal is not to glorify our reading ability, but to glorify God through accurately reading His message.
      2) Reverence: "When we read the Bible carelessly and without expression, how can we expect the impressionable youths in the congregation to develop a sense of reverence and awe for the Bible?" (McComiskey 15).
      3) Revelation: "If when we read the Bible to an audience, we read it carelessly, with little concern for its message or beauty, we dull its impact" (McComiskey 15).

2. PROCEDURE: Memory glue: **READING**
   a. **R**EAD aloud several times considering the following:
      1) Exaggeration: Exaggerate emphasized words, emotions, and punctuation pauses in order to impress them on your mind.
      2) Conversation: Re-read it in a conversational tone without exaggeration.
      3) Articulation: Speak clearly.
         a) Finish words. Sound out letters like "d," "t," and "g" at the end of words.
         b) Don't run words together. "Mon" is not the proper way to say "come on."
      4) Pronunciation: Say words and especially names correctly.
         a) Some editions of the Bible can aid with this (have accent marks, tell when vowel is long or short, etc.).
         b) Bible encyclopedias and dictionaries can help.
         c) There are Bible pronunciation books as well.
         d) Listening to audio Bibles can assist pronunciation.
         e) Taking time to pronounce words and names properly impresses the audience with the importance we give to the reading of the passage.
         f) If you cannot find a proper pronunciation of a name then decide on one and say it with confidence.
         g) Worry more about how the name is pronounced today than how it was pronounced in the past.

We are not trying to astound the audience with our knowledge. We want them to know whom it is we are reading about. If possible, use the pronunciation they are used to.

It is okay to talk to them after the reading about how the name might have been stated in Bible times, just don't make such a big deal of it that it detracts from Scripture.

      5) Memorization:
         a) SECRET: If you want to memorize your text, involve as many of the senses as possible.
         b) SEE: Read over your text silently several times.
         c) SPEAK: Read the passage aloud.
         d) HEAR: Listen to an audio file of someone reading the passage in the version you are using.
         e) TOUCH: Write the verses, not looking at the text.

1. Go as far as you can without looking.
2. When you hit a road block, reread the text.
3. Repeat this until you can write it completely from memory.

    f) TASTE:
1. Practice saying the text from memory until you can go all the way through it.
2. Once you can do this then you have "tasted" and consumed the text. It is part of you.

b. **E**YE CONTACT:
1) Pick up your Bible (this aids with eye contact and projecting your voice).
2) Place your Bible about one foot from your face, but do not cover your face (it will muffle your sound).
3) Put your finger where you are reading to keep your place.

c. **A**CTING: Bring it to life.
1) Portray the emotions of the text with slight facial expressions as well as head and body movements.
    a) The audience may not see this, but it will help you.
    b) Be careful with gestures.
        1. They can draw attention from the text.
        2. You may knock the Bible from your hands.

2) Positioning of your head can show a change in speaker.
    a) Turn slightly to the left for one speaker.
    b) Turn slightly to the right for another speaker.

3) Power should be added to your voice to emphasize key words, exclamation points, etc.

4) Pitch is a potent tool.
    a) Slight raising or lowering of the pitch of your voice can aid in showing emotion and character change.
    b) Do not over-do this. Remember that you are trying to draw attention to the text, not yourself. You do not want to sound like you are on Broadway, but you also do not want to be monotone.

5) Pace is important as well.
   a) Speeding up can show excitement, confusion, rapid movement, etc.
   b) Slowing down can show deep emotion, sincerity, the somberness of the setting, mystery, etc.
   c) Read your passage at a slower pace than you normally speak.
      1. This allows the audience to follow along.
      2. This allows you to speed up without going too fast for the audience.

6) Pausing is a tremendous aid in showing punctuation..
   a) Pause longer for periods, colons and semi-colons than for commas.
   b) Pause without taking a breath at commas.
   c) Pause and take a breath for periods, colons, and semi-colons.

d. **D**ETERMINE the basics of the passage.
   1) Who is the author, and audience?
   2) What is the setting and central thought of the passage?
   3) Which words need to be emphasized?
   4) What contrasts need to be brought out? (Example: "You have heard . . .but, I say").

e. **I**NDICATE: Mark the text in your Bible.
   1) You might use a paper clip, book mark, or a piece of paper.
   2) Keep it neat. A Bible with papers sticking out in all directions gives the appearance of disorganization.

f. **N**OTICE the road signs.
   1) Notice words like "therefore," "because," or "for."
      a) These tell you that something important is coming.
      b) These often need to be emphasized with the voice and/or a pause.
   2) Notice periods and commas. Remember that a Bible verse may start in the middle of a sentence.
   3) Notice exclamation points and question marks and reflect them with your voice.

g. **G**LANCE: Learn to read ahead.
   1) Learn to catch words, phrases, and sentences at a glance.
   2) This aids in eye contact. If your mind contains the entire sentence, you can look up at the audience in the middle.

THE UNIFORM

Major league uniforms identify which team each player is playing for. They can also become a source of embarrassment. Steve Lyons played for four major league teams from 1985-93. He is now a television commentator. He once slid head-first into first base during a game. Naturally his pants were filled with dirt. Forgetting where he was, he pulled his pants down to get the dirt out. Needless to say, it was a rather embarrassing moment. That is one more reason why he was known as "Psycho." Many know him more for that instance, than for what he did as a player. For the preacher, our clothing can either accentuate the sermon or distract from it.

A. SHOW: Our clothing tells the audience about us.
   1. It tells them if we consider worship and preaching to be important.
   2. It tells them if we are organized and self controlled.

B. SETTING:
   1. Dress should fit the audience and the setting.
      a. Sometimes being overdressed can be as bad as being underdressed.
      b. Speaking at a wilderness retreat in a button-down suit might not be the most effective way to reach the audience.
   2. Generally, it is better to be overdressed than underdressed.
   3. Discuss the appropriate attire with the leaders where you are speaking.

C. STANDARD: Generally speaking, you should dress as well or better than the best dressed person in your audience. Be an example that others can follow.

D.   SPECIFICS:
1.   Generally, wear a suit and tie on Sunday mornings and Sunday nights. On Wednesday nights you should wear at least a dress shirt and tie.
2.   Comb your hair, brush your teeth (put peppermints in your coat pocket), and shave your face (or neatly trim your beard).
3.   Keep your tie straight and tight. It is a good idea to have a handkerchief.

PRE-GAME WARM-UP: TAKING CARE OF YOUR VOICE MUSCLES

Major leaguers warm up their muscles before the game. You will see them out on the field taking batting practice, making long tosses, and running sprints. Our vocal cords are muscles and must be warmed up and cared for as well. The following is drawn largely from a video entitled The Vocal Coach Speaker's Workshop by Chris Beatty.

A.   ABDOMEN Breathing: Breath from the waist, not the chest. This allows you to maintain more control of your breath. Practice controlling your breath by breathing in and counting to five as you breath out.

B.   ABUSES of the voice:
1.   Not WARMING UP: Humming or singing can be helpful. You can also do the bubble exercise (blowing through your lips while humming). It is good to do warm-ups in the shower (this is a warm, moist area). It is also good to do these same things to warm-down the voice as well.

2.   ICING UP: Never have ice cold liquids on the podium when speaking (defeats purpose of warming up voice, causes vocal cords to draw up). Drink room-temperature water during speaking.

3.   DRYING UP: Keep vocal cords moist. The body is constantly losing moisture (cf. breath on a cold day). Speaking adds to this problem. Drink 8-10   eight ounce glasses of water per day. There are also throat sprays. Use a spray   which moistens, not one that numbs (just hides the problem).

4.   USING UP: Don't over-drive the voice (cf. using car as a truck). It was not built for screaming or over-use (especially in the cold). It needs rest.

5.   BREAKING UP: Don't clear your throat. It causes the vocal cords to slam together (cf. small children do not clear their throats).

6. SPEAKING UP in an unnatural voice. Speaking too high or too low puts strain on your voice. Most speak below their optimum speaking pitch. Saying "uh huh" naturally with your mouth closed will show you your optimum speaking pitch. You might also find the lowest note you can match with your voice on a piano keyboard and move up 5 notes.

Robert Redford plays the character of Roy Hobbs in the movie, *The Natural*. It is a movie about a baseball player that comes out of nowhere to become a legend. Hobbs uses a bat made from a tree struck by lightning to hit mammoth homeruns. He called his bat Wonderboy and carried it in a special case to protect it. Our voices are like Roy Hobbs' special bat. They are the key to our success in spreading God's Word. We cannot carry our voices in a special case, but it is very important that we take care of them.

DON'T SHOW UP THE PITCHER: WORD CHOICE

A classy ball player will go out of his way not to "show up" a pitcher. Some players run the bases slowly, do a dance, or dangle an arm while running after a home-run. Pitchers do not appreciated this. Similarly, we must not "show up" the audience by using words they do not understand. Word choice is important in effective speaking. If we choose to use big words, we may show our arrogance more than our intelligence.

A. PRONUNCIATION:
   1. This is to "say a word in the manner accepted as correct" (Kougle 108).

   2. If we fail in pronunciation and/or articulation people may:
      a. Not understand our words.
      b. Think we are not intelligent.
      c. Think the lesson was unimportant to us.
      d. Think that we are unprepared.

   3. A standard Dictionary, some editions of the Bible, Bible encyclopedias and dictionaries, and Bible pronunciation books can help with this.

   4. Be careful with people's names.
      a. Ask them or someone who knows them to pronounce their name.
      b. You might write the pronunciation phonetically with accent marks.

   c. Example: You might write "Mike Piazza" as "Mike Pi aht' sa."

B. ARTICULATION:

  1. This is "the formation and production of the individual sounds that make up language" (Kougl 108). It is the art of speaking clearly.

  2. Finish words. Sound out letters like "d," "t," and "g" at the end of words.

  3. Don't run words together. Say, "Do you want some?," not, "Ont sum?"

C. CLARIFICATION
Use clear words that people can understand. "All of our teaching must be as plain and evident as we can make it. If you would not teach men, what are you doing in the pulpit. If you would, then why do you not speak so as to be understood?" (Baxter 118).

  1. SIMPLE: Use simple words and sentences. The shorter the distance between the bases, the faster the runner covers the distance. The shorter the distance from the beginning of our sentences to the end, the faster the message reaches the audience.

  2. SIGNALS: Avoid technical terms. Define difficult words. A third base coach may give signals which the batter understands, but they mean little to the fans. Don't use big words which mean nothing to the audience.

  3. SPECIFIC: Use specific words. When outfielders are calling for a fly ball they are very specific in what they say, so as to avoid a collision. We must use specific words which best describe what we are trying to say.

  4. SLANG: Avoid slang words. They are generally used by small groups and quickly change in meaning. Define terms you must use (cf. Kougle 109).

  5. SENSITIVE: Avoid euphemisms, slurs, sexist/racial comments, and off-color jokes. They are inappropriate for a child of God and offensive.

D. VIVIDNESS: Use vivid words that bring the message to life. Jesus did this when he said, "Hunger and thirst for righteousness." Create word pictures.

E. GRAMMAR: Poor grammar hinders our credibility. Notice especially your use of verb tenses ("The wind blew" instead of "The wind blowed") and your noun/verb agreement (nouns and verbs must agree in number: "They were," instead of "They was"). Watch slang grammar such as "I et," instead of "I ate."

THE CRACK OF THE BAT: THE PREACHER'S VOICE

There is nothing like the cracking sound that echoes through the ballpark when the bat cleanly strikes the ball. There can also be nothing like the quality sound of a preacher's voice as he preaches the Word. Yet, the sound of his voice can also destroy his message.

A.   PITCH:

    1.   SNORE: Your voice needs to be flexible (avoid monotone which bores).

    2.   SHOW
        a.   Pitch can show if something is a QUESTION or a STATEMENT.
            1)   Example: My teacher asked, "Are you going to turn in your paper today or tomorrow?" I answered, ("Today./Today?").
            2)   If the answer is "Today," then you would say it normally.
            3)   If the answer is "Today?" then you would raise the pitch of your voice so as to show that you can't believe that the teacher wants it today.
        b.   Pitch can show a change in SPEAKER when reading (slightly raise or lower your pitch).
        c.   Pitch can show if you are SERIOUS or joking.
        d.   Pitch can show EMOTION (increase pitch to show excitement or lower your pitch to show sincerity, sadness, etc.).
        e.   Pitch can show a PARENTHETICAL phrase (slightly lower pitch).

    3.   SHRILL
        a.   PLEASANT: Your voice should be pleasant (no harsh shrill).
        b.   PALATE: Lifting the palate in the roof of your mouth (yawning sensation) can aid in giving the voice a pleasant sound.

    4.   SEEK your optimum pitch (see #6 above under "Abuses of your voice").
        a.   NATURAL: Your voice should be natural and not an artificial "preaching voice."
        b.   CONVERSATIONAL: Have a conversation with the audience.
        c.   PERSONAL: Be yourself, do not imitate others.

B.   POWER

1.   STRONG: Be loud enough to be heard, but not so loud that it hurts the audience's ears or your voice.
    a.   LUNGS: Force more air out of your lungs to increase volume.
    b.   LOWER pitched voices tend to project farther. Drop your pitch slightly when you want to increase your volume (cf. Kougl 110).
    c.   LIFT: Concentrate on raising the palate in the roof of your mouth (the sensation you feel when you yawn).
        1)   This allows the sound more room to resonate and can aid in increasing volume.
        2)   If you speak from the back of your throat it makes your voice sound hollow and speaking from the front of your mouth makes it sound pinched. Both decrease the volume.
        3)   Avoid opening the back of the throat too much. It makes your speech too breathy and decreases its strength.
    d.   LAST: Many start strong and then fade at the end of sentences or thoughts to a point that people cannot hear them. Concentrate on not letting your voice tail off.

2.   STRESS key words to show capitals, bold face, exclamation points, etc.

3.   SECURE audience's attention by making your voice louder.
    a.   This needs to be varied. If you are loud the whole sermon, the effect is lost.
    b.   Sometimes a loud whisper is more effective than a shout.

C.   PACE

1.   SLOW: Do not speak so slowly it is boring or so fast they cannot follow.
2.   SHOW:
    a.   Slowing your rate emphasizes words and thoughts.
    b.   Slowing your rate can show deep emotion, seriousness, sadness and mystery.
    c.   Speeding up your rate can show excitement, confusion and rapid movement.
3.   SMOOTH: Avoid stammering.
    a.   Words like "uh" are verbal crutches and destroy the sermon flow.
    b.   These "crutches" may cause people to think you are unprepared.
    c.   These "crutches" can become annoying to the audience.

       d.   Transition statements between points can aid with smoothness ("Having considered the person on the cross, now let us turn our attention to the purpose of the cross").

D.   PAUSE

1. CURIOSITY: Pausing gets attention. If you stop, they will look up.
2. CONTEMPLATION:
    a. It allows the audience time to think and feel about a point.
    b. It allows you time to think.
        1) If you have forgotten what comes next, don't say "uh."
        2) Pause and think. Some silence is good. Remember the silence seems longer to you than it does to the audience.
        3) Repeating your last sentence in slightly different words or a quick review of you points may trigger your memory.

3. CENTER STAGE:
    a. Pausing before or after (or both) a statement emphasizes it.
    b. Pausing can emphasize emotion.
    c. Pause long enough to draw attention to the key word or point, but not so long that you draw attention to the pause.

4. COMMAS: Pausing shows punctuation (periods, exclamation points etc.).

DON'T MISS FIRST: THE PREACHER'S MANNERISM

Just after hitting his 62nd home run, Mark McGwire leapt into the arms of Cardinals' first base coach Dave McKay. He was so excited that he completely jumped over first base in the process. Here is one of the most memorable moments in sports history and he misses first base! Likewise, many a great sermon has been rendered less effective by a preacher's mannerisms.

A. MAN: Stand straight and tall as you speak.
    1. SEE: People see you before they hear you.
    2. SAYS: Our posture says we are bored, excited, tense, etc.
    3. STAND with your head balanced over your shoulders, knees, hips, and ankles.
        a. cf. Habits of a 15 month old child.
        b. Don't drape yourself over the podium or lean on it.

   c. Do not stand like you are in the army with your chest forward and your shoulders back. It puts strain on the body.

   d. Imagine that your are being gently lifted from behind your ears.

  4. If SITTING, you should feel like you are standing from the waist up (cf. Beatty).

B. MAINTAIN good eye contact. It is important for a batter and a fielder to keep their eye on the ball in order to be effective. Likewise, we must keep our eyes on the audience in order to be effective.

  1. SHOW: Eye contact shows sincerity, attracts attention, and allows you to get feedback from the audience. If someone has a puzzled look on their face, then you may need to explain something further.

  2. SIMPLIFY: If you write out a complete manuscript, do not read it from the pulpit or memorize it. Reduce it to outline form before preaching it.

  3. SHADE: I find that it helps me to highlight the key parts of my outline. I highlight the title, intro, conclusion and main points in yellow, sub-points "A, B, C" in blue, illustrations in pink, and scriptures in green. This causes them to "leap" off the page if I have to use my notes.

  4. SINGLE: Try to make personal eye contact with as many individuals as possible. If the congregation is large, look at a small group at a time.

  5. SURVEY the entire audience. Do not stare at just one or two sections.

  6. SHOULDER: If you are too nervous to look people in the eye, look at their shoulder or at a space between two people. Work to improve this ability.

C. MOVEMENT

  1. MOVEMENT attracts attention, brings the message to life, communicates emotions, aids in understanding, emphasizes points, builds a rapport with the audience, and releases nervous energy. "A preacher needs to carry over into preaching the same freedom he gives to his hands, arms, and head in personal conversation. . . . we should not gesture less in the pulpit than we do in private" (Robinson 198).

  2. MECHANICAL: Make sure they are natural, not mechanical.

   a. They should flow from the message, not be programed into it.

b. Use the normal gestures you would use in everyday speech.

3. METHOD: Express the emotions of the sermon by:
   a. Using facial expressions (smile, furrowed brow, etc.).
   b. Using your eyes (widening, narrowing, etc.).
   c. Using body movements (palms upward when expressing uncertainty, stepping back and pausing to show the end of a point, or stepping slightly to the side for a new point, etc.).

D. MANNERISMS: Avoid the following which distract from the message.

1. SCOLDING: Don't scold the audience by shaking your finger.

2. EXAGGERATING: Don't over-exaggerate. Gestures should draw attention to the sermon, not away from it.

3. ANNOYING: Avoid the following habits which annoy the audience.
   a. A hand in your pocket jingling keys.
   b. Standing on one leg.
   c. Nervous pacing.
   d. Rocking back and forth.
   e. Rubbing your ear, constantly adjusting your glasses, etc.
   f. Showing your notes. Be as discreet as possible when changing pages in your notes (no loud shuffling of pages). Shrinking your notes and paper clipping them in you Bible can help.

E. MOTIVATED: Be excited about your message. You can often tell when a player is into the game or when he is just going through the motions. Likewise, people can tell by our voice and body language if we are sincere and excited about our messages. They will likely not be motivated unless we are.

1. EXCITEMENT is contagious. Psyche yourself up like before a ball game.

2. EXCESS: Don't overdo it. If you are nervous, then they will be (rub the back of your neck or hide a yawn to relax).

3. ENCOURAGEMENT: Remember that you are more prepared to preach that sermon than anyone.

REMEMBER THAT YOU ARE MORE PREPARED TO PREACH THAT SERMON THAN ANYONE.

CROSSING THE PLATE. REMEMBER WHY YOU'RE HERE, TO SAVE SOULS.

I remember watching a highschool baseball game in which a player hit a home run. There were other runners on base and one of them failed to touch home plate. Fortunately for him, the umpire did not notice. A home run is wasted if we fail to touch home plate. A sermon is also wasted if we fail to "call people home."

John Broadus notes that there are three goals to every sermon: (1) Pleasing God, (2) Saving souls, and (3) edifying "the church and helping his people to mature" (50). We must keep these goals ever before us. Fewer and fewer sermons include the plan of salvation. Make it a part of your sermons. It can come in the beginning, middle or end (be original). We must inspire people to come to God in the invitation. Remember that our goal is to bring people "home" to God (Mtt. 18.11). Our goal is not to glorify ourselves or our preaching ability. We seek to inspire people to glorify God.

THE WELCOME COMMITTEE: HANDLING RESPONSES

A player is often mobbed by his teammates when he crosses home plate after a home run. We also know that the angels in heaven rejoice when a lost child of God "comes home." It is important that we properly welcome those who respond to the invitation. We have adopted a "No one responds alone" policy where I preach. A friend comes forward to sit by them.

A.   RECONNAISSANCE: Plan ahead.
　　　1.   Talk to the Elders, Preacher, or person who invited you to speak and find out who is handling responses. Also, ask which elder would like to lead a prayer for those rededicating their lives. If you are handling the responses, have someone prepared to help in the event there are several responses. Ask if there is anyone who helps the baptismal candidates get dressed. Make sure the baptismal pool is clean and warm.

　　　2.   If you are handling responses, ask if there are response cards. If they have none then get some index cards and write "Name" and "comments" on it. We are all prone to forget. It is helpful if the person responding will write their name and a brief summary of their needs. This is also helpful to the church secretary for announcing the response in the bulletin.

　　　3.   Make sure the baptismal clothes, towels, and waders are ready.

B. RESPONSE: Handling the response.

    1. Stand at the front of the auditorium and scan the crowd for people who might respond. Notice people's faces. You can often tell who is thinking about coming forward. Note those who seem to be deliberating but do not respond and offer them an encouraging word after the services.

    2. Greet warmly those who respond. Show genuine excitement. Be very careful about how you hug women!

    3. Those responding are making themselves vulnerable (support them).

    4. Hand them the response card and a pen or pencil.

    5. While they are filling out the card, step back to the front of the auditorium. I do this because many people will not come if no one is there to receive them. One response often inspires others.

C. REDEDICATION:

    1. If a person is rededicating his/her life, offer them encouragement and let them know you will be praying for them (don't say it if you don't mean it). Let them know that they are starting over with a clean slate. Ask them if they would like to talk with you or someone else after services.

    2. Go to the pulpit, announce the persons name, and read their response. Congratulate them for their courage. Challenge the audience to examine themselves and to befriend the brother or sister who has responded.

    3. Ask the person (elder etc.) who you made previous arrangements with to lead the prayer (or lead it yourself).

    4. I often encourage the person responding to go to the back of the auditorium so the members can hug and congratulate them on the way out.

D. REBIRTH: Baptisms.
    1. QUESTIONS: If a person responds wanting to be baptized, there are some questions which must be asked. Here are some possible approaches:

	a.	Why do you want to be baptized?

a. Why do you want to be baptized?
b. What will happen to you spiritually when you are baptized?
c. What will happen if you are not baptized?
d. Do you believe that Jesus Christ is the Son of God?
e. Are you willing to confess that Jesus is God's Son?
f. Do you understand what it means to repent?

2. CAUTION: If their response lets you know that they need to study more:
   a. Then set up a time after services when you (or someone else, if need be) can study with them.
   b. Tell the audience that the person responding has come forward wanting to become a Christian and that the two of you are going to be studying together.
   c. Ask the congregation to be praying about the study.

3. CONVERSION: If they are ready for baptism:
   a. Announce their desire to the audience.
   b. You can take their confession at this point (I do it in the pool).
      1) Ask them if they believe Jesus Christ is the Son of God.
      2) I know one preacher who asks, "What do you believe?"
   c. Ask them to go get dressed. Make sure there is someone who can help them with baptismal clothing and towels.
   d. Ask the song leader to lead songs until you are ready (ask him to stop when he sees you enter the baptismal pool).
   e. Once both of you are dressed, briefly walk the candidate through the baptismal process before conducting the baptism.
      1) Ask if they are afraid of water. Some will be. Reassure them. If they are afraid, tell them you can have another man in the pool to assist you if it will reassure them.
      2) Ask them to grasp their right wrist with their left hand (if they are right handed). You must grasp both the hand and wrists of the candidate (this keeps their arms from flailing). Place your other hand in the middle of their back.

      3) Tell them what you are going to say, "Based upon . . ."
      4) Tell them to cover their mouth with their hand at this point and act as if they are falling backward in a chair. Remind them that you want to get them completely under, so they

will not stick their hands or feet up in the air. Tell them to stand up when they feel you lift upward against their back.

    f.   Once you feel like they understand, proceed with the baptism.

1)   You need to enter first and help them in.

2)   I am right handed so I baptize to my left.

3)   I have them stand facing my right (I face the audience if it is a left to right pool and I have hem face the audience if it is a front to back pool).

4)   Get their hands in position. Grab their hand/wrist with you right hand and place your left in the middle of their back.

5)   Make sure that you are to the far right of the pool (if baptizing to the left) so you will not strike their head on the wall or steps on the other side.

6)   Your right foot should be even with their feet or slightly in front of them. Your left foot should be behind them. This allows your left foot to support them when you lay them back and keeps them from pulling you over on them.

7)   Take their confession (if you have not already done so).

8)   Tell them, "Based upon your confession I am honored to baptize you in the name of the Father, the Son, and the Holy Spirit for the forgiveness of your sins and you will receive the gift of the Holy Spirit" (or something similar, Acts 2:38).

9)   Push their hand up to their mouth and lean them back.

10)   Look to make sure that you get them completely under.

11)   Lift them out of the water (pushing with left hand and foot and lifting with the right hand on the wrist).

12)   Hug them and welcome them to the family of God.

13)   Make arrangements for the Lord's supper (if on a Sunday).

14)   Make arrangements for follow-up contact.

15)   I encourage people to write down how they felt and why they were baptized. They will enjoy reading it in years to come. If they ever wonder whether they did it for the right reasons, they will have it written down. They will also be able to share their story with others who are thinking about baptism.

16)   P.S. This is not the only baptismal method that is effective. I have a friend that basically just has people go straight down in a bent position to baptize them. I just tried to share the method I use.

CONCLUSION

I like to play fantasy baseball. Everyone needs physical and mental recreation that helps them to relax. Fantasy sports helps with my mental relaxation. I usually have two Yahoo teams each summer. You can learn a lot about baseball by being the manager of a fantasy baseball team. It also allows you to keep up with your favorite teams and players. Yet, as much fun as fantasy baseball is, it is not the same as actually going out and playing baseball. You might view this workbook as a fantasy-preaching league. It allows you to learn about and practice developing and delivering a sermon. The next section (Batting Practice) outlines the process of putting a sermon together and leaves blanks for you to fill in the necessary information. This process can assist your efforts to learn sermon preparation and presentation. Yet, it is not the same as actually going out and preaching. I challenge you to look for opportunities to put what you are learning into practice. Constantly watch for opportunities to speak for the Savior. It is time to make fantasy reality!

SECTION TWO
BATTING PRACTICE

TOPICAL SERMONS

WHAT TO SAY

TOPIC:

TEXT:

PASSAGES, INVENTORY, and COMMENT: Review Bible passages on your topic and pick out the ones you feel will help you discuss your topic in the best way (use a Concordance or Topical Bible). Write a summary of each verse you choose beside it.

KEY: From these verses pick the verse you feel will be the best key text for your sermon.

WHAT IT SAID

MEANING: Define key words in your text and words you do not understand. Note if they are used as a noun, verb etc. (Use Vine's Dict., Robertson's Word Pictures etc.).

EXPLORE: Use your concordance to see how the key words are used elsewhere in N.T. and write a summary by them (words like "forgiveness," "faith" etc.).

SETTING:
WHOLE BOOK CONTEXT: (commentaries and intro books):
Who wrote the book your text is in?
Who did he write it to?
Why did he write it?

What type of literature is it (historical book, a letter, poetry etc.)?

WHERE DOES IT FIT IN HISTORY: (Use customs books, commentaries, Bible dict.).
What is the date? (If we are able to know the date, this is optional)

Is there a major historical event or social circumstance that must be considered? (i.e., the conflict between Jews and Samaritans, or the persecution under Nero etc.).

Consider what kings, rulers, or customs might effect the verse (i.e., "foot washing" etc).

WHAT WRAPS AROUND THE TEXT: Note the verses before and after your text.
Who is speaking?
Who is he speaking to?
What event is taking place?

What verse and chapter does the discussion/event start with?
What is discussed in the verses and paragraph before your text?

What is being discussed in the verses and paragraph after your text?

What type of literature is it (key verse might be a story, poem etc.)?

SUBJECT MATTER: Write in a complete sentence what you feel your text is about.

APPLY AGAIN and GIST: Look back at the other verses you found in your concordance search (page 41). Make sure you know MEANING of the key words and the SETTING of these parallel passages. Record this information below. List the passages below and write their main point beside them (you only do this with the verses you plan to use).

EXAMINE: Write down any relevant comments made by Bible scholars about your text and/or parallel passages (see commentaries, articles, sermons etc.):

WHAT IT SAYS

WRITE and ORGANIZE: Write 2-5 main points on your subject from your list of parallel passages and group all the information you have gathered under the appropriate point (each passage stresses a different aspect of your topic, these aspects can become points):

1.

2.

3.

4.

5.

RELEVANT: Eliminate passages or material that are not necessary (take your pen or pencil and erase or cross-out the unnecessary information in the section above):

LIGHT and DO: Add any explanations or observations which will aid in understanding each point and then apply each point to your audience:

1.   Point:
Explanations and observations:

Application:

Point:
Explanations and observations:

Application:

Point:
Explanations and observations:

Application:

Point:
Explanations and observations:

Application:

Point:
Explanations and observations:

Application:

HOW TO SAY IT

STORIES: Write any illustrations (stories, poems, quotes etc.) that will help with memory and motivation on each point.

1.

2.

3.

4.

5.

PREPARE INTRODUCTION AND CONCLUSION:

INTRODUCTION:
Illustration: Write down any Stories, poems, quotes, interesting statements, visual aids or current events that relate to the theme of the text and get attention:

Background: Write any relevant background information that you feel would be appropriate in the introduction (Theme of book, author of the book etc.).

Thesis: Write a complete sentence that summarizes the goal of your sermon.

CONCLUSION:
Action: What action do you want the audience to take? (How do they put the topic you have discussed into action? What do they need to do differently?)

Illustration: Write an illustration which can help the audience remember your sermon and will motivate them to take action.

Salvation: List the plan of salvation with Scripture references.

ATTENTION:

TITLE: Write an interesting title for the sermon that gets attention and fits the theme.

POINTS: Word your main points so that they are interesting and easy to remember (alliteration, same letter of alphabet, rhyme, catchy phrase etc.).

1.

2.

3.

4.

5.

NOTES: Place all this information in the appropriate place in your outline.

EXPOSITORY SERMONS

WHAT IT SAID ("MESSAGE").

MEANING: Define the key words (i.e., "faith," "forgiveness," etc.) in your text and any words you do not understand (i.e., "propitiation" etc.) (use Greek word-study books like Vine's, an English dictionary and compare translations - Focus on the Greek meaning).

EXPLORE: Use your concordance to see how the key words in the text are used elsewhere in the New Testament. List the most helpful verses below.

SETTING:
WHAT IS THE WHOLE BOOK CONTEXT?: (Intro books and Commentaries).
What is the theme of the book your text is from?
—

Who wrote it?
Who did he write it to?
Why did he write it?

What type of literature is it? Is it a story, poem, parable etc.? (Commentaries can help).

WHERE DOES IT FIT IN HISTORY?: (Use customs books, commentaries, Bible dict.).
What is the date of the events in the verse? (If we are able to know the date, optional)

Is there a major historical event or social circumstance that must be considered? (i.e., social issues like the treatment of women or Jew/Gentile relations).

Consider what rulers, or customs might affect the verse (i.e., crucifixion practices etc.).

WHAT WRAPS AROUND THE TEXT: Note the verses before and after your text.
Who is speaking?
Who is he speaking to?
What event is taking place?

What verse and chapter does the discussion/event start with?
What is discussed in the verses before and after your text?

What type of literature is it? (story, poem etc.)
Other important features of these verses:

SUBJECT MATTER: Write in a complete sentence the main idea of your text.

APPLY AGAIN and GIST: Find other Bible verses which are relevant to the theme of your text (i.e., If your text is about faith, look up "faith" in your concordance. You may have already found these verses in your previous word search). Summarize their message and how they apply to your theme. Make sure you know the meaning of the words and setting for these passages (you only need to know this for the verses you plan to use).

EXAMINE: Examine what qualified Bible scholars say about your text and list the helpful comments below (commentaries, articles, sermons etc.):

WHAT IT SAYS ("WORLD")

WRITE and ORGANIZE: Write 3 to 5 main points from the text which elaborate on the theme and group all the information you have gathered so far under the appropriate point (i.e., you might use the verbs in your text as your main points; cf. "repent," "turn," "do" in Acts 26.20).

1.

2.

3.

4.

5.

RELEVANT: Eliminate any unnecessary information (mark it out of the section above):

LIGHT and DO: Add any observations/explanations that shed light on the points and then apply each point (i.e., you might observe from Acts 26.20 that repentance should always lead to action).

1.   Point:
Observation or explanation:

Application:

2.   Point:
Observation or explanation:

Application:

3.   Point:
Observation or explanation:

Application:

4.   Point:
Observation or explanation:

Application:

5.   Point:
Observation or explanation:

Application:

HⓄW TⓄ SAY IT ("SPAN").

STORIES: Write any Bible and/or modern day illustrations, quotes, statistics, poems, visual aids etc., which will help the audience to understand and remember your points (use quote books, illustration books, articles, every day life etc.).

1.

2.

3.

4.

5.

PREPARE an introduction and conclusion:
INTRODUCTION:

Illustrations: Write down any stories, poems, quotes, interesting statements, visual aids or current events that relate to the theme of the text and get attention:

Thesis: Write a complete sentence that summarizes the goal of your sermon.

Background: Write any relevant background information that you feel would be appropriate in the introduction (theme of the book, author of the book etc.).

CONCLUSION:
Action: What action do you want the audience to take in light of your text?

Illustration: Write an illustration which can help the audience remember your sermon and will motivate them to take action.

Salvation: List the plan of salvation with Scripture references.

ATTENTION:

TITLE: Write an interesting title for the sermon that gets attention and fits the theme.

POINTS: Word your main points so that they gain attention and are easy to remember (alliteration, same letter of alphabet, rhyme, catchy phrase etc.).

1.

2.

3.

4.

5.

NOTES: Place all this information in the appropriate place in your outline.

PARABLE SERMONS

WHAT IT SAID ("MESSAGE").

MEANING: Read the parable in different translations and define key words and words you do not understand (i.e., "forgiveness," "propitiation," "trust" etc.; Use Vine's etc.).

EXPLORE: Read other accounts of this parable, noting differences between them and also ways the other accounts help you understand your text.

SETTING:

WHOLE BOOK CONTEXT: (Intro books and Commentaries).
What is the theme of the book?

Who wrote the book?
Who did he write it to?
Why did he write it?

WHERE DOES IT FIT IN HISTORY? (Customs books, dictionaries, commentaries etc.)
Are there rulers, events, social issues that affect the parable? (i.e., Samaritan relations).

Are there customs you need to learn more about? (Farming, slavery etc.).

WHAT WRAPS AROUND YOUR PARABLE? (The IMMEDIATE CONTEXT):

Note the verses before and after the verses you are studying.

Who is speaking?
Who is he speaking to?
What caused this parable to be told? (question, argument etc.)

What follow-up comments by the person telling the story can be helpful? (i.e. Mt 18.35).

SUBJECT MATTER: Write in one sentence what you see as the parable's central point.

APPLY TO N.T. and get the GIST: Note what other Bible verses have to say about your subject (forgiveness, kindness etc.), and list the helpful ones below. Make sure you have the basic meaning or "gist" of these passages and write it beside them.

EXAMINE: Read comments by Bible scholars on the parable you are considering and write the helpful comments below (commentaries, sermons, books on parables etc.).

WHAT IT SA⬚S ("WORLD").

WRITE and ORGANIZE: Write 2 to 5 main points from the parable which will allow a framework for discussing its theme and then group all the information you have gathered under the appropriate point (i.e., point one might deal with the circumstances of the parable, point two might focus on details of the parable and customs, and point three might focus on applying the parable).

1.

2.

3.

4.

5.

RELEVANT: Eliminate any unnecessary information from the section above.

LIGHT and DO: Add any observations/explanations that shed light on the points and then apply each point to your audience (i.e., "What do they need to do or learn?").

1.   Point:
Observations and explanations:

Application:

2.   Point:
Observations and explanations:

Application:

3.   Point:
Observations and explanations:

Application:

4.   Point:
Observations and explanations:

Application:

5.	Point:
Observations and explanations:

Application:

H◻ W T◻ SA◻ IT ("SPAN").

STORIES: Write any Bible and/or modern day illustrations, quotes, statistics, poems, visual aids etc., which will help the audience to understand and remember your points (use newspaper articles, every day life, quote books, illustration books, etc.).

PREPARE an introduction and conclusion:

INTRODUCTION:
Illustrations: Write down any stories, poems, quotes, interesting statements, visual aids or current events that relate to the theme of the text and get attention:

Thesis: Write a complete sentence that summarizes the goal of your sermon.

Background: Write any relevant background information that you feel would be appropriate in the introduction (theme of the book, author of the book etc.).

List anything else you think would be appropriate in the introduction (such as why it is important to discuss this parable).

CONCLUSION:
Action: What action do you want the audience to take?

Illustration: Write an illustration that helps the audience to remember your sermon and will motivate them to take action.

Salvation: List the plan of salvation with Scripture references.

ATTENTION: Reword your title and main points so as to get attention.

TITLE: Write an interesting title for the sermon that gets attention and fits the theme.

POINTS: Word your main points so that they are easy to remember (alliteration, same letter of alphabet, rhyme, catchy phrase etc.).

1.

2.

3.

4.

5.

NOTES: Place all this information in the appropriate place in your outline.

CHARACTER SERMONS

1.   ACCESS scriptures on your character.
Look up his/her name in a concordance or character study book and list the verses.

2.   ANALYZE:
        Take Out Bible: Read each of the passages listed above and write a summery of each.

3.   ASSESS the verses you have found.
What you want to teach about your character from these verses?

Make a simple outline (organize verses under your points/eliminate unnecessary ones).

Point one:

Point two:

Point three:

Point four:

Point five:

4.   APPLY steps of Take Me Out to the Ballgame to the verses you plan to use.

TAKE OUT BIBLE: Read three versions of each and write what you learned.

LEARN ABOUT CROWD: Study setting of each book that has verse on your character. Who wrote each book and to whom did they write it?

What is the theme of each book?

What problem/s is each book dealing with?

STUDY CUSTOMS (PEANUTS AND CRACKER JACK):
What customs affect the verse?

What type of literature is the book each verse is in? (narrative, law, poetry, etc)

GO BACK TO HISTORY: What is the historical background of the verse?
Are there dates, events, or social issues relevant to each verse?

Are there rulers, or political issues which are relevant to each verse?

What customs/world events might affect the understanding of each verse?

ROOT FOR WORD MEANINGS: Define the words in each verse you do not know or you think are important.

SHAME NOT TO CONSIDER SETTING: Note the setting surrounding each verse. Where does the discussion begin that each verse is a part of?

What comments before or after each verse might aid in understanding it?

Who is the speaker and audience for each verse?

What events or problems cause the discussion/events that each verse is part of?

What type of literature is each verse? (See commentaries, intro books)

CHECK "OUT" OTHER WRITERS: Consider what others have to say on each verse. Bible writers (use your concordance to look up key words such as "faith" etc.).

What do commentaries, sermons, articles say about each verse?

What do character study books, encyclopedias/dictionaries etc. say about your character?

GAME: Give Author's Meaning Expression: Summarize main point/s of each passage.

5.   ADD illustrations.
Introduction:

Point one:

Point two:

Point three:

Point four:

Point five:

Conclusion:

6.   AUDIENCE APPLICATION: Apply each point.

Point one:

Point two:

Point three:

Point four:

Point five:

7.   ADJUST for final preaching form.

Do you need to make any adjustments to your points or sub-points? (You may decide to eliminate items or to rename your title or points to aid attention and memory).
Title:

Point one:

Point two:

Point three:

Point four:

Point five:

OUTLINE: Place this information in the appropriate place in your outline.

OUTLINE

Title: _____

Text: _____

Thesis:

Introduction:
1.   Illustration.

2.   Relevant background information.

3.   Relevance of the topic to people's lives.

4.   Introduce main points.

I.	Main Point: _____. (You do not have to use all of the following. These are examples of the types of things you use to build points)

A.	Relevant terms and definitions.

B.	Relevant Bible passages.

C.	Relevant background info.

D.	Observations, explanations or restatement of thoughts in other words.

E.	Application.

F.	Quotes, statistics or illustrations.

II.   Main Point: _____. (You do not have to use all of the following. These are examples of the types of things you use to build points)

A.   Relevant terms and definitions.

B.   Relevant Bible passages.

C.   Relevant background info.

D.   Observations, explanations or restatement of thoughts in other words.

E.   Application.

F.   Quotes, statistics or illustrations.

III.   Main Point: _____. (You do not have to use all of the following. These are examples of the types of things you use to build points)

A.   Relevant terms and definitions.

B.   Relevant Bible passages.

C.   Relevant background info.

D.   Observations, explanations or restatement of thoughts in other words.

E.   Application.

F.   Quotes, statistics or illustrations.

IV.   Main Point: _____. (You do not have to use all of the following. These are examples of the types of things you use to build points)

A.   Relevant terms and definitions.

B.   Relevant Bible passages.

C.   Relevant background info.

D.   Observations, explanations and restatement of thoughts in other words.

E.   Application.

F.   Quotes, statistics or illustrations.

V.   Main Point: _____. (You do not have to
use all of the following. These are examples of the types of things you use to build
points)

A.   Relevant terms and definitions.

B.   Relevant Bible passages.

C.   Relevant background info.

D.   Observations, explanations or restatement of thoughts in other words.

E.   Application.

F.   Quotes, statistics or illustrations.

Conclusion:

1.   Review main points.

2.   Illustration which reminds and motivates.

3.   How does the audience make its life right with God (Baptism, rededication)?

4.   What action should the audience take in light of your text/subject/character?

THE FRAGRANCE OF CHRIST
Matt. 18.21-35

INTRO:

1. Mark Twain said, "Forgiveness is the fragrance that the flower leaves on the heel of the one who crushed it" (Edyth Draper).

2. This fragrance should be in the life of God's people, "And be kind to one another, tenderhearted, forgiving one another, just as God in Christ forgave you" (Eph. 4:32 NKJ).

3. Yet, this is easier said than done. When you feel the pain of another's boot, the last thing you want to do is forgive. How do you put the hurt aside? How do you swallow your pride and forgive? The answer is . . . "Jesus." Let us turn to Matthew 18 and see what Jesus can teach us about forgiveness. We will use the letter "S" as our memory glue as we focus on SEVEN, STORY, SELF and SAVIOR.

I. SEVEN (Mtt. 18:21-22).

   A. Our Questions:
      1. If someone killed a member of your family, could you forgive them?
      2. Do you have someone who has caused you great pain and anguish?
      3. Is it hard to think about them without becoming upset?
      4. Do they say they are sorry and then hurt you again?
      5. Do you find yourself saying, "How long do I have to go on forgiving them? They don't care about me. How much is enough?"

   B. Peter's Question (Matt 18:21-22).

      1. Peter's question was probably prompted by Jesus' discussion concerning how to respond to a brother/sister who sins (cf. Matt. 18:15-20).

2. Did Peter have someone specific in mind who had sinned against him?

3. Some scholars say the Rabbis taught people to forgive others seven times. Other scholars say the Rabbis only required people to forgive three times. Either way, Peter wasn't asking for less than the Rabbis required.

4. Jesus said 490 times. He is not saying we should have a chart on our refrigerator door with 490 squares and mark off one each time someone sins against us. Jesus' message was we should keep on forgiving.

II. STORY (Lk. 18.23-34).

A. The Story:
1. Jesus drove his point home by telling a story (parable).
2. Summarize the story told in verses 23-34 in your own words.

B. The Specifics:

1. The servant owed 10,000 Talents (6,000 danarii in a Talent).
   a. One danarius was a day's wages for unskilled labor.
   b. Would have had to work 60,000,000 days to pay off.

2. The other servant owed 100 danarii.
   a. Could pay off in 100 days (approx. 4 months).
   b. Ratio between what each owed was 600,000 to 1.

3. This probably made 70 X 7 look good (cf. Word In Life Bible, 1674-75).

III. SELF (Matt. 18.35).

A. A couple married for 15 years began having more than usual disagreements. They wanted to make their marriage work and agreed on an idea the wife had. For one month they planned to drop a slip in a "Fault" box. The boxes would provide a place to let the other know about daily irritations. The wife was diligent in her efforts and approach: "leaving the jelly top off the jar," "wet towels on the shower floor," "dirty socks not in hamper," on and on until the end of the month. After dinner, at the end of the month, they exchanged boxes. The husband reflected on what he had done wrong. Then the wife opened her box and began reading. They were all the same, the message on each slip was, "I love you!" (Bible Illustrator).

B.   We are called to forgive as he forgave (Eph. 4:32; Col. 3:12-13; Titus 3:1-7).

    1.   We were treated better than we deserved (cf. parable of servant - Mtt. 18).

    2.   We are to treat others better than they deserve.
    3.   Crete, where Titus worked, was an sinful place. Yet, the brethren were to treat those around them with kindness because God had shown them mercy and (cf. Titus 3.1ff).

C.   We are forgiven as we forgive (Matt. 18:35; Matt. 6:12, 14-15).

    1.   God forgives us accordingly (Matt. 18.35).

    2.   So does man (cf. "when his fellow servants saw" - Matt. 18.31).
    3.   We often want people to overlook our faults, but we are harsh with others.
    4.   Forgiveness blesses the giver and the receiver.

        a.   The Receiver has the burden of guilt lifted.
        b.   The giver has the burden of bitterness lifted and will be treated more compassionately by God and others.

IV.   SAVIOR.

A.   Jesus practiced what he preached (Acts 1:1; Matt 23:1-4).

B.   Jesus showed Peter how to practice the teaching of the parable.

    1.   Peter saw forgiveness portrayed before him on the cross (Luke 23:33-34).
    2.   Peter experienced it personally after the resurrection (Mk 16.7; John 21).

C. In spite of suffering, Jesus forgave.

   1. Would you forgive if "12 legions of Angels" were waiting to help you? Jesus felt the boot heel of the world, but left the fragrance of forgiveness.

   2. When Narvaez, the Spanish patriot, lay dying, he was asked whether he had forgiven all his enemies. Narvaez looked astonished and said, "I have no enemies, I have shot them all." (Bible Illustrator).

CONCLUSION:

1. There's a Spanish story of a father and son who had become estranged. The son ran away, and the father set off to find him. He searched for months to no avail. Finally, in a last desperate effort to find him, the father put an ad in a Madrid newspaper. The ad read: "Dear Paco, meet me in front of this newspaper office at noon on Saturday. All is forgiven. I love you. Your Father." On Saturday 800 Pacos showed up, looking for forgiveness (Bits & Pieces, Oct. 15, 1992, p. 13).

2. The world is filled with people looking for forgiveness. Will they find it though us?

3. Are you seeking a God who forgives and forgets? (Jer. 31.35). [Give plan of salvation]

THE ONE THAT DIDN'T GET AWAY

INTRO:

1. A ship was going down at sea in a storm. The Captain asked, "Is there anyone here who knows how to pray?" One of the sailors responded, "Aye Captain." "Good," said the Captain, "You start praying and we'll put on the life vests. We are one short" (Blair).

2. I love to fish. It is fun to talk about the big fish that got away. You never really know how big it was, but it sure is fun to wonder. This lesson focuses on the biblical story of a ship caught in a mighty storm and the "big fish" who didn't let a prophet get away.

3. Is it a true story?
    a. Some say it is a myth while others say it is an allegory.
    b. It is in fact a true story.
        1) Jonah is a real prophet (2 Kings 14:25).
        2) Christ stated it was a real story (Matt. 12:39-41; 16:4; Lk. 11:29-30).
4. Jonah was the son of Amattai.
    a. From Gath Hepher, a town just north of the road to Tiberius and 2 miles from Nazareth (International Standard Bible Encyclopedia).
    b. He was from the tribe of Zebulon.
    c. He was a prophet to the Northern Kingdom of Israel.
    d. He seems to have prophesied during the reign of Jeroboam II (793-753 B.C.).
5. The letter "A" will be our memory glue as we focus on ACTION and APPLICATION.

I. ACTION.
    A. Running from God (chapter 1).

        1. Asked by God to go to Nineveh (largest heathen city in the world).

        2. Fled to Tarshish by way of Joppa.
            a. Tarshish: "In Spain, at the farthest west, at the greatest distance from Nineveh in the northeast" (Jamieson, Fausset, and Brown).

        b.   Joppa: This was the port for those going to and from Jerusalem. It is where Peter healed Tabitha and it is where he was when sent for by Cornelius (Acts 9-10).

3.   Asleep in the ship.
      a.   Maybe conscience did not bother him.
      b.   May have believed God would take care of him anyway.

4.   Like the Captain in story we told at the beginning of this lesson, the Captain of Jonah's ship asked them to pray. They cast lots to see who was at fault. Jonah told them to cast him overboard. The men rowed to keep from throwing Jonah overboard. They finally threw Jonah in.

5.   Men prayed not to be blamed. They sacrificed after delivered and feared the Lord (something good can even come from something bad).

6.   Fish (do not know what kind) sent by God to swallow Jonah.

B.   Running to God (chapter 2).

1.   Joe Louis was the world heavyweight boxing champion from 1937 until he retired in 1949. In 1946 Louis prepared to defend his title against a skilled fighter named Billy Conn. Louis was warned to watch out for Conn's great speed and his tactic of darting in to attack and then moving quickly out of his opponent's range. In a famous display of confidence, Louis replied, "He can run, but he can't hide" (Today in the Word, 7-6-93).

2.   Can you imagine being in a fishes belly? (smells bad enough on outside!)

3.   Jonah learned that you can't hide from God.

4.   He repented and prayed in the belly of the fish (2:7-9).

5.   The fish vomited Jonah out.

C.   Running with God (chapter 3).
    1.   Went to Nineveh (3:3)
        a.   Literally: "Great city to God." Jews saw all things in light of God.
        b.   3 days in size:
            1.   A fast walker could walk 60 miles in three days. We do not actually know what standard the writer went by. He does not specify how many miles a day's walk was.
            2.   The writer also does not specify if walking straight through, around the outside, or walking through the middle and stopping to speak periodically as a prophet would.
            3.   The actual walled portion was about 8 miles in circumference. The suburbs extended well beyond the walled portion of the city.
        c.   It was a city of at least 120,000. This number may refer only to children who "do not know right from left" - Jonah 4:11 (ISBE).
        d.   He walked in a days journey. We do not know his route. Would have stopped often to speak.
    2.   Warned them they would be destroyed in 40 days (3:4).

        The people believed and repented (3:8-9).
        They sat in sackcloth and ashes.
        The king participated and made a decree that all should mourn.

D.   Running ahead of God (chapter 4).
    Jonah was displeased and angry.
    Reason Jonah fled is revealed (4:2-3).
        a.   He knew they would repent.
        b.   He knew God would forgive. He wanted them punished.
        c.   They were a cruel people hated by many Jews.

    3.   He built a shelter to see what would happen and God sent a plant to shade him from the sun. When I lived in Israel in the summer of 1987 I came to understand the heat of the noonday sun. In modern Israel they close many of the shops during the heat of the day and reopen them when it is cooler.

    4.   God sent a worm to kill the plant. Jonah begged to die.

5.   God teaches Jonah that he has more concern for a plant than lost people.

II.   APPLICATION.
    A.   FOCUS is on Jonah and God. Little is said about Nineveh's repentance.

    B.   FOREIGNERS: The book shows the Gentiles in a very positive light.

        1.   Notice the positive examples.
            a.   Sailor's sought to save Jonah's life.
            b.   The sailors offered sacrifices and prayers when delivered.
            c.   The Ninevites believed and repented.
        2.   The Assyrians (Nineveh) were already a threat to Israel and would be responsible for its destruction in 722 B.C.
        3.   Their repentance stands in stark contrast to Israel's sin and may be the reason that they played a hand in Israel's destruction.

    C.   FATHER: Lessons learned from God in the story.
        1.   God loves all people (it does not matter what the skin color is).
        2.   God is merciful to Jonah, Nineveh, and to all who repent.

    D.   FORGIVENESS: Lessons learned from Jonah in the story.
        1.   We cannot hide from God.
        2.   We must not reject another's genuine repentance.
            a.   Jonah was a good and devout man.
            b.   Yet, he was vengeful and unforgiving.
                1)   Like brother of prodigal son (Lk. 15:28-32).
                2)   Like those jealous of the 11th hour workers (Mtt 20:9-16).
                3)   We should be grateful for anyone's repentance (2 Pet. 3:9).

        3.   The Word is powerful, even when it comes from a reluctant preacher (Ph. 1:18; Rm. 1:16).

CONCLUSION:
    1.   This book is highly regarded by the Jews. It was chosen as the special portion of Scripture to be read on the day of Atonement when the High Priest went into the Most Holy Place of the Temple. It should be important to us as well (ISBE).

    2.   A telemarketer called a home one day, and a small voice whispered, "Hello?"

"Hello! What's your name?" Still whispering, the voice said, "Jimmy."
"How old are you, Jimmy?" "I'm four."
"Good, Is your mother home?" "Yes, but she's busy."
"Okay, is your father home?" "He's busy too."
"I see, who else is there?" "The police."
"The police? May I speak with one of them?" "They're busy."
"Any other grown-ups there?" "The firemen."
"May I speak with a fireman, please?" "They're all busy."
"Jimmy, all those people in your house, and I can't talk with any of them? What are they doing?"
"Looking for me," whispered Jimmy (The Jokesmith, qtd in Bits & Pieces, 4-1-93, 3-4).

3.   If God is looking for us, it is no laughing matter.

4.   The people of Nineveh will bear witness at the Judgement against those who reject the teaching of Christ (Matt. 12:41).

5.   Will we repent or run? Give the plan of salvation (believe, repent, confess, baptize).

6.   Do we have good reason to do what we do? (Jonah 4:4, 9).

SCRIPTURE READING PRACTICE

A.   Read these verses noticing that verse 9 divides a sentence. Also observe pauses at periods, commas and semi-colons. Pause longer for periods and colons.

Psalm 98:8-9

8 Let the rivers clap their hands, Let the mountains sing together for joy
9 Before the LORD, for He is coming to judge the earth;
He will judge the world with righteousness
And the peoples with equity. NASU

B.   Learn the pronunciation of the names and places in these verses and read the verses aloud, pronouncing them properly.

Titus 3:12-13

12 When I send Artemas or Tychicus to you, make every effort to come to me at Nicopolis, for I have decided to spend the winter there.
13 Diligently help Zenas the lawyer and Apollos on their way so that nothing is lacking for them. NASU

C.   Read this passage putting special emphasis on expressing the emotions of the passage.

1.   Express the sorrow and heartbreak of Mary's weeping and questions.
2.   Express Mary's frustration of not knowing where Jesus is.
3.   Express the concern in the voice of the Angels and Jesus (i.e., "Why are you weeping?").
4.   Express Mary's joy as she says, "Rabboni!"

John 20:11-18

11 But Mary was standing outside the tomb weeping; and so, as she wept, she stooped and looked into the tomb;

12 and she saw two angels in white sitting, one at the head and one at the feet, where the body of Jesus had been lying.

13 And they said to her, "Woman, why are you weeping?" She said to them, "Because they have taken away my Lord, and I do not know where they have laid Him."

14 When she had said this, she turned around and saw Jesus standing there, and did not know that it was Jesus.

15 Jesus said to her, "Woman, why are you weeping? Whom are you seeking?" Supposing Him to be the gardener, she said to Him, "Sir, if you have carried Him away, tell me where you have laid Him, and I will take Him away."

16 Jesus said to her, "Mary!" She turned and said to Him in Hebrew, "Rabboni!" (which means, Teacher).

17 Jesus said to her, "Stop clinging to Me, for I have not yet ascended to the Father; but go to My brethren and say to them, "I ascend to My Father and your Father, and My God and your God.'"

18 Mary Magdalene came, announcing to the disciples, "I have seen the Lord," and that He had said these things to her. NASU

D.   There are several items to notice in this passage.
    1.   Remember to reflect your commas, periods and semi-colons with pauses.
    2.   Reflect your sign-post words with added emphasis, "therefore," "for," "but," "and," "because" etc.
    3.   Notice words and phrases that are connected with "and." Bring this out in your reading.
    4.   Reflect the question marks with your voice.
    5.   Reflect the contrast in verses 7 and 8:
        a.   Paul is saying that he will reward people according to their deeds.
        b.   He contrasts two types of people.
            1)   "to those who by perseverance in doing good seek for glory and honor and immortality,"
            2)   "but to those who are selfishly ambitious and do not obey the truth, but obey unrighteousness,"
        c.   He contrasts two rewards as well.
            1)   "Eternal life."
            2)   "wrath and indignation."
        d.   The word "but" and a pause at each of the commas and periods are important in bringing out these contrasts.

Rom 2:1-8

1 Therefore you have no excuse, everyone of you who passes judgment, for in that which you judge another, you condemn yourself; for you who judge practice the same things.

2 And we know that the judgment of God rightly falls upon those who practice such things.

3 But do you suppose this, O man, when you pass judgment on those who practice such things and do the same yourself, that you will escape the judgment of God?

4 Or do you think lightly of the riches of His kindness and tolerance and patience, not knowing that the kindness of God leads you to repentance?

5 But because of your stubbornness and unrepentant heart you are storing up wrath for yourself in the day of wrath and revelation of the righteous judgment of God,

6 who WILL RENDER TO EACH PERSON ACCORDING TO HIS DEEDS:

7 to those who by perseverance in doing good seek for glory and honor and immortality, eternal life;

8 but to those who are selfishly ambitious and do not obey the truth, but obey unrighteousness, wrath and indignation. NASU

ARTICULATION PRACTICE

Ezio Pinza's (singer at the Metropolitan Opera) favorite was, "Three gray geese in the green grass grazing; gray were the geese, and green was the grazing."
Actor Laurence Olivier often warmed up with this one before going onstage: "Betty Botter bought a bit of butter, 'But," she said, 'this butter's bitter. If I put it in my batter, it will make my batter bitter. But a bit of better butter will make my batter better.' So Betty Botter bought a bit of better butter, and it made her batter better."

Boris Karloff lisped, and the letter "s" was his problem. Among the twisters he used were: "She sells seashells by the seashore"; "Sister Susie's sewing shirts for soldiers"; "Slippery sleds slide smoothly down the sluiceway" ; "A snifter of snuff is enough snuff for a sniff for a snuff sniffer."

A twister used by some radio and television announcers before they perform is: "The seething sea ceaseth and thus the seething sea sufficeth us."

Nine out of 10 people can't say this twice in rapid succession: "Sinful Caesar sipped his snifter, seized his knees and sneezed." (Frederick John, Insight, qtd. in Blair).

*Make the distinction clear in the following (Carnagie, Public 180):
bust-buzz
cease-seize
face-phase
hiss-his   mace-maize
most-mosey
muscle-muzzle
puss-puzzle

PAUSE AND POWER PRACTICE
(Stafford North, Church 14)

**Emphasize underlined words and pause at /.
1.   Every member of the church/ must be a worker.

2.   Prayer/ can change your life.
       Prayer can/ change your life.
       Prayer can change/ your life.
       Prayer can change your/ life.
       Prayer can change your life.

3.   I believe that Jesus Christ/ is the Son of God.
       I believe that Jesus Christ is/ the Son of God.

4.   I am going to be a better Christian. Will you?

5.   Today/ is the day of salvation.

6.   He that believes and is baptized/ shall be saved.

7.   So then faith comes by hearing/ and hearing/ by the Word of God.

PITCH PRACTICE

*Say the word "no" in the following examples so as to convey these different meanings (Kruger 51):

"No–you don't say so" (incredulous).
"No–absolutely not" (firm refusal).
"No–I don't think so" (doubt).
"No–it's really no trouble" (friendly).
"No–not especially" (polite, matter-of-fact refusal).
"No–don't jump" (pleading, urgency or fear).

VOICE QUALITY PRACTICE

*Say "ah" and listen to the sound. Then, say "ah" while pinching your nose. If the sound changes then you are probably resonating too much in your nose and not enough from the palate in the roof of your mouth. Practice saying all the vowels (a, e, i, o, u) while alternating pinching and not pinching your nose until there is no change in the sound (cf. Kruger 48).

ACCENT PRACTICE

*Consider the stress (or accent, shown by capitalization) of the following words:
ADdress (noun)
FInance (noun)
INcrease (noun)
EXport (noun)   adDress (verb)
fiNANCE (verb)
inCREASE (verb)
exPORT (verb)

PRONUNCIATION PRACTICE

*Do not say (Carnagie, Public 94):

except for accept
ailmunt for ailment
ambassadur for ambassedor
becuz for because
ejucation for education
cramberry for cranberry
fillum for film
forchin for fortune
genl'mun for gentlemen
guvement for government

SECTION THREE
THE BULLPEN

THINGS TO CALL ON WHEN NEEDED

The Call

"Then He said to His disciples, 'The harvest is plentiful, but the workers are few. Therefore, beseech the Lord of the harvest to send out workers into His harvest'" (Matt. 9:37-38).

These words are even more relevant today than they were in Jesus' day. We live in a world of over 6 billion souls and many have never heard the name of Jesus. "Each minute 99 people die somewhere in the world; many die lost" (J. J. Turner). A study by the Barna Research Group shows that "ninety-three percent of all Americans own at least one Bible, and most own more than one." A poll by George Gallup shows that eight in ten Americans claim to be Christians, but half do not know who preached the Sermon on the Mount. Only three out of five could name the first four books of the New Testament. The Barna study showed that thirty-nine percent did not know that Jesus was born in Bethlehem (Blair). Even in America, in what is supposed to be a "Christian nation," people do not know the Word of God. Truly the harvest is plentiful. While it is true that the harvest is plentiful, it is also true that the laborers are few. "We average losing two preachers each day. During 1995 we lost an estimated 800 preachers while during the same year all our schools combined trained approximately 200 preachers" (J. J. Turner). The need is greater, but the number of men willing to devote their lives to the spreading of God's Word is quickly diminishing. In our congregations we are also seeing fewer and fewer men who are willing to take on leadership roles. The professional world calls our brightest minds away from the pulpit and, sadly, parents often encourage it. If we do not change this trend, then the consequences could be deadly. Someone took the time to teach us. Will we take the time to teach others? Who will answer the call? A major league pitcher may receive a "call" from his coach to come into the game and pitch. How does a person know if he is "called" to preach? The following is the result of a couple of papers I was asked to do for graduate classes in 2003 and 2006. They challenged me to consider why I felt I should preach the Gospel. I pray the following thoughts will challenge you also.

The Call

K. L. Schmidt states that the Greek term kaleo "may always be rendered 'to call,' but often has the special nuance of divine calling or vocation" (1985, 394). John Polhill notes that the terms "call" and "called" are primarily used in the New Testament in a general sense. He states, "This calling is God's invitation to share in the salvation offered through Christ" (1996, 66). The exception to this would be Paul who was "called to be an apostle, separated to the gospel of God" (cf. Rom. 1:1; 1 Cor. 1:1 New King James Version). Paul's call to salvation and his call to ministry actually took place at the same time (cf. Acts 9, 22, 26). All Christians are called to salvation and gifted for service (cf. 1 Cor. 12:13ff; Rom. 12:1-8; Eph. 4:11-16). Yet, some are called to special forms of ministry as Paul was called to the unique task of apostolic ministry. While the term "called" is not a term used in the Bible for ministers or evangelists in general, it can serve to describe the sense that one is in ministry because God wants him to be there. William Willimon states, "Although [preachers] may struggle with exactly what it means to be called by God to lead a church, they must have some sense that they are in ministry because God wants them to be" (14). This section will proceed with that definition of "calling" in mind. Yet, How does a man know if ministry is what God wants him to do?

Timothy's Life

Paul was "called" to ministry; yet, his call was a very dramatic call to a very unique ministry (apostle). Ministers today do not expect to see a bright light or hear a voice from heaven to let them know they have been called. Timothy might be a better subject for analysis. He and Titus may be the closest New Testament comparisons to the ministerial vocation as it is know and practiced today. Timothy was the son of a pagan father and a believing mother (Acts 16:1, 2 Tim. 2:15). Paul probably led Timothy to Christ during his first missionary journey (Acts 14:6; 1 Tim. 1:2). Timothy was a known co-worker of Paul (Tit. 1:5, 1 Tim. 1:3, 2 Tim. 2:15; Acts 17:14, 18:5, 19:22; 20:4). His name is found in six of Paul's epistles as a fellow sender. Timothy was sent, on occasion, to individual communities to carry out special responsibilities (1 Thess. 3:2, 6; 1 Cor. 4:17; 16:10; Phil. 2:19-23). Prior to writing First Timothy, Paul had left Timothy to work with the church at Ephesus while Paul himself traveled on to Macedonia. It seems that there was a problem with false teachers at Ephesus. Paul wrote the letter to guide the brethren in Ephesus and to remind Timothy of his responsibilities as a "minister of Jesus Christ" (1 Tim. 4:6).

Timothy's Ministry

The term translated as "minister" in 1 Timothy 4:6 is the Greek term diakonos. It means "a helper or a servant, and is sometimes translated 'minister'" (UBS 2004, CD ROM). It is used 30 times in the New Testament and 18 times by Paul (Englishmans 2004, CD ROM). In Paul's writings it used with reference to Jesus Christ (Rom. 15:8), Satan's servants (2 Cor. 11:15), governments (Rom. 13:4), Paul and his co-workers (1 Cor. 3:5-6), and the office of deacon (1 Timothy 3:8ff). Paul seems to use it of "servants" who carry out specific tasks for another. Paul identifies the tasks of Timothy's ministry as follows: godly example, public reading of Scripture, teaching/instruction, and commanding/exhortation to obey God's message. Timothy can serve as an appropriate subject for comparison when considering the call of modern Christians to ministries related to the proclamation of the Word.

Timothy's Calling

One might begin this exploration of Timothy's calling by considering a statement Paul made to him in First Timothy 3:1, "If any man aspires to the office of overseer, it is a fine work he desires to do." Note the term "desires" in this passage. This text refers to the office of elder. An elder will inherently be involved in proclamation of the Word (Titus 1:9-10) but a person may be a preacher and not serve as an elder. Thus, this passage does not apply directly to preaching. Yet, it is reasonable to assume that if a man is going to serve in the Lord's work there must be a desire present to do so or at least a willingness to do so whether it is as an elder, preacher, or both. Some have a burning passion to proclaim the message (1 Cor. 9:16). Others may have more reluctance (cf. Moses in Exodus 3-4). Timothy seems to have suffered from timidity; yet, he was willing to serve (cf. 2 Tim. 1:7). Thus, calling requires an inner call, an inner desire or at least a willingness to serve as a minister of the Gospel. This inner call may grow out of such motivations as love for God's people (cf. Phil. 2:20) and/or awareness that there is a need to share God's message with a lost world (cf. 2 Tim. 4:2-4). Others may influence this desire/willingness. Timothy was influenced by his family (2 Tim. 1:5), a Christian mentor (2 Tim. 3:10-11), and by the brethren in his community (Acts 16:2). Timothy not only had a willingness to serve, but was given gifts by God to be able to do this ministry (2 Tim. 1:6). Paul and the local brethren were able to help Timothy to assess his gifts and his ability to serve as a minister (2 Tim. 4:5; 1 Tim. 4:14). Paul challenged Timothy to pay careful attention to his lifestyle and teaching (1 Tim. 4:12, 16). Thus, these factors are obviously important if one is called to ministry. Finally, Timothy received an outer call or appointment to service by a congregation of God's people (Acts 16:2; 1 Tim. 4:14). William Willimon felt that this "outer call" was more reliable than the individual's inner call (1990, 95ff). It serves to confirm or validate the inner desire/willingness. Based on the call of Timothy, one might summarize the call to ministry as follows:

1. Call from Within (Inner call): Having an inner desire/willingness to serve.
2. Call from Above (Higher call): Having gifts or ability from God to do ministry.
3. Call from Without (Outer call):
   a. Conduct - Having a godly lifestyle above reproach.
   b. Comment - Assessment of one's fitness for ministry by faithful Christians.
   c. Community – Appointment to a ministry by a Christian community.

Looking for these elements can help each of us to determine if God is calling us to preach.

My Call

My call began with my parents. My dad is a mechanical engineer but he also preached for about fifteen years when I was growing up. He modeled ministry as well as love for God and people before me. He led training classes for the young men in the congregations that we worshiped and worked with. He exposed me to preacher training camps at Freed-Hardeman University in Henderson, Tennessee and the Pennington Bend church of Christ in Nashville, Tennessee. My mother was a constant example and source of encouragement. Local congregations also gave me the opportunity to preach on a regular basis while I was in high school. Out of this grew a tremendous love for telling people about Jesus. The Future Preacher's Training Camp in Nashville helped to solidify my decision. W. K. "Pete" Johnson and the camp staff helped me to see the tremendous need for Gospel preachers who would "seek and save the lost" (Lk. 19:10). Brother Johnson often said, "God only had one son and he made him a preacher." When I first attended the camp I was planning to be a lawyer and to preach "on the side." During the camp that summer I decided that there was nothing more important that I could do than preach the Gospel. I reached for the plow in July of 1982 and have never looked back.

Influences

Like Timothy, I have many influences that help me to believe that God wants me to tell others about Jesus. I have an inner desire to minister. I love to tell people about Jesus. I want as many people in heaven as possible. I love the look on people's faces when they come to an understanding of something in God's Word for the first time. I want desperately for people to see the difference that God can make in their lives. While I feel inadequate in many ways, I feel that my talents and desires are suited for ministry. I like people and enjoy teaching and preaching. Family members, mentors, and brothers and sisters in Christ have encouraged me to use the gifts God gave me. Finally, specific congregations have called me to service. These are the reasons why I feel that this is what God wants me to do. I constantly pray that God will continue to open the door of ministry, if this is how he wants me to serve him.

Motivation

I also preach because three primary motivations. First of all, Jesus was a preacher (Mark 1:14, 38-39). We have salvation because he came, preached, and died for our sins (John 3:16). What better can I do with my life than to imitate the Son of God. A second reason to preach is that someone took the time to teach us. The world cannot believe if no one tells them the message of salvation (Rom. 10:14). Someone taught us the Word of God. Don't others deserve to know what we know? Pass it on. The third foundational reason I preach is that the world needs Christ. The world is dying in sin. It is sick and needs help (Isa. 59:1-2; Eph 2.1-3; James 1.13-15). There is a message that can save them. If we do not tell them then we are like a doctor who does not treat a patient and the patient dies. We have a message that can save people's souls (Rom. 1:16; 2 Tim 3.16-17). We must share it.

Passion

I preach because the Word is "a fire in my bones and I cannot hold it back" (Jer. 20:9). It would break my heart if I could not share God's message with others. If I lost my voice I would have to find some way to teach with my hands or through written words. Paul told Timothy, "Do not neglect the spiritual gift within you." I believe I would be neglecting the gift that God has given me if I did not preach. I recognize both that there are many others who can do this work and that I have inadequacies and faults. Yet, I believe that God can work through my life to save souls, bring glory to his name, and make a difference in the world. As long as there is breath in my chest or until God guides me in a different direction, I shall endeavor to preach the Gospel.

Conclusion

Most major league teams have a phone line which runs from the dugout to the bullpen where the relief pitchers warm up before entering the game. The coach uses this phone line to call for a new pitcher. Has God called you to enter his work? Apply the elements of calling listed above to your life, seek the input of your spiritual mentors, and pray diligently that God will help you make the right decision. If you sense that God is "calling" you to be a minister of the Gospel, are you willing to answer the call?

THE BUNT

Devotional Talks

1. There will be times when it is not necessary to hit a home run in order to win a game. Sometimes a bunt is all that is needed to bring home the winning run.
2. Likewise a minister may be called upon to deliver a short devotional talk of 3-5 minutes.
3. The following is drawn largely from Dale Carnegie's book Effective Speaking (117-138).
4. Carnegie calls this the "Magic Formula" for "Making the Short Talk to Get Action."

I. Preaching/Teaching can make a difference in people's lives.

American president, Abraham Lincoln said, "He who molds public opinion goes deeper than he who makes laws." In other words, what we do in shaping peoples minds through preaching the Word of God is more important than making the laws of a nation. J.D. Jones (an English preacher), was encouraged to run for the house of commons. In his letter of response he quoted Nehemiah, "I am doing a great work and I can't come down." He underlined "come down" twice. Preaching God's message was the most important thing he could do. Many jobs keep people alive (doctors, policemen etc.), but the preacher's message makes their life worth living (2 Cor. 4.5). We have a unique opportunity. We can say each week what can change lives forever (Billy Smith).

   A. We must take this responsibility very seriously. Richard Baxter (1615-1691, Puritan preacher and chaplain in Oliver Cromwell's army) said, "I preach as if I will never preach again, as a dying man to dying men. As a man betwixt living and dead" (118). We should not make preaching trivial. American president Woodrow Wilson said, "The only profession that consists in being something is ministers of our Lord Jesus Christ and nothing else."

William Quayle said, "Preaching is the art of making and delivering a sermon; no, preaching is the art of making and delivering a preacher" (The Pastor-Preacher). In other words, our lives and character are part of our sermons. Second Corinthians 4:5

says we "preach Christ." We need to make sure that Christ is not hidden behind our poor character. We need to be a window through which the light of Christ shines. If the window is dirty or smudged, the light is hindered. Most books on preaching, stress character more than anything else. We preach two sermons each time we preach: (1) What our words say, and (2) What our character says (Billy Smith).

      B.   Don't start thinking too highly of yourself. The authority by which we preach is not our own. Our authority is from the Lord.

      C.   NT metaphors of the preacher (cf. John Stott, Between Two Worlds, pp.135-137).

            a.   Herald: (An announcer). The most common in NT. It is a town crier who called all together and delivered announcements for the King (I Cor. 1.23).

            b.   Sower: Planted now, sprouts later (Luke 8.4). Little things plant a seed.

            c.   Ambassadors: (II Cor. 5.20). Probably talking here about the apostles. But we too have been commissioned as emissaries.

            d.   Steward: He is entrusted with a house. We are stewards of the mysteries of God (I Cor. 4.1-2). We must be faithful. We must not leave the truth and turn to human opinions.

            e.   Shepherd: Protecting the flock from wolves. The elders are entrusted with this (Acts 20.28-31), but they use us to carry it out.

            f.   Workman: (II Tim. 2.15). "Handle aright" means literally to "cut straight." We need straight teaching of truth. Examples: Nathan to David, Jesus to the lawyer.

            g.   These metaphors emphasize the "givenness" of the message. We do not create it. Good news has been given to the herald and good seed to the sower. We are servants under the authority of another.

II. **Three "S" Devotionals:** (Based on principles in Dale Carnegie's book Effective Speaking (117-138). Carnegie calls this the "Magic Formula" for "Making the Short Talk to Get Action."

      A.   Illustration/Story: Begin with a story from your personal experience or chose an illustration which will gain attention and applies to the point of your devotional.

            1.   Start your talk with your example (jump right into the story).

2.   Saturate your story with relevant details.

3.   Submerge yourself in the story. Relive your experience as you relate it.

B.   Application/Significant point: "State your point, what you want your audience to do."

     1.   Precise: Make the point brief and specific.

     2.   Powerful: State the point with force and conviction.

     3.   Point out: Show people what they need to do in light of your point.

C.   Motivation/Scripture: "Give the reason or benefit the audience may expect."

     1.   Benefit: Show people how they will benefit from acting on the point.

     2.   Bible: The Bible is the main reason we do what we do.

         a.   The point must be supported by and flow from scripture. Select a passage or two that best support the point of your devotional.

         b.   Do not just stick a scripture on your story or illustration like a post-it note someone sticks on a refrigerator. The scripture you choose should be the basis and foundation of your message. Your story should illustrate, explain, and/or draw attention to your key scripture.

         c.   Make sure you use the verse within its context or setting.

     3.   Be sure the reason is relevant to the example.

D.   Summarization:

     1.   Begin with an illustration.

     2.   Make your point and tell them what they need to do.

     3.   Tell them why they should do what you are asking them to do.

     4.   Remember that this is a devotional, not a full sermon.

a.   Don't try to make six points and quote the whole Bible.

b.   It aids memory to have one illustration, one point and one key scripture.

1.   What is the purpose of public speaking? Dale Carnegie's lists several in his book, Effective Speaking. The preacher may find his summary helpful.

2.   The purpose must fit the occasion and the audience.

I.   Making the short talk to get action.
   A.   Give your example, an incident from your life.
   B.   State your point, what you want your audience to do.
   C.   Give the reason or benefit the audience may expect.

II.   Making the talk to inform.
   A.   Restrict your subject to fit the time at your disposal.
   B.   Arrange your ideas in sequence.
   C.   Enumerate your points as you make them.
   D.   Compare the strange with the familiar.
   E.   Use visual aids.

III.   Making the talk to convince.
   A.   Win confidence by deserving it.
   B.   Get a yes-response.
   C.   Speak with contagious enthusiasm.
   D.   Show respect and affection to your audience.
   E.   Begin in a friendly way.

IV.   Making impromptu talks.
   A.   Practice impromptu speaking.
   B.   Be mentally ready to speak impromptu.
   C.   Get into an example immediately.
   D.   Speak with animation and force.
   E.   Use the principle of the here and now.
   F.   Don't talk impromptu–give an impromptu talk.

Conclusion

Some times we may wonder if the lessons we teach are making a difference. We must remember that our lessons are like drops of rain that nourish the earth. They go into people's hearts and slowly but surely they help them grow closer to the Lord. What if no one taught? A man wrote a letter to a large newspaper complaining that he had heard many sermons, but could not remember one. Another man wrote back the next week to respond to the first letter. He said, "My wife has prepared many meals. I remember few of them, but I am healthy." People may not remember every sermon we preach, but little by little the message nourishes those who listen. Let us make sure we are feeding people good spiritual food.

"If you study the ads you see in magazines and newspapers and on television and analyze their content you will be amazed at how often the Magic Formula is used to persuade people to buy" (Carnegie 138). This formula can also aid the minister in delivering short talks.

THE PLAY-BOOK

The Preacher's Library

VERSIONS (Compare Three, Prefer Committee Translations)

- Updated New American Standard
- English Standard Version
- New King James Version
- New International Version
- King James Version
- Revised Standard Version
- American Standard Version
- Harmony of the Books of Samuel, Kings, and Chronicles by William Day Crockett
- A Synopsis/Harmony of the Gospels

CONCORDANCE (Most Important Tool Next to Your Bible)

- Strong's Exhaustive Concordance of the Bible
- Cruden's Concordance
- Young's Analytical Concordance
- Naves Topical Bible
- The Treasury of Scriptural Knowledge

ENCYCLOPEDIA / DICTIONARIES / ATLASES

- International Standard Bible Encyclopedia (revised), ed. by Geofrey W. Bromiley
- Nelson's Bible Dictionary
- New Unger's Bible Dictionary
- The Lion Encyclopedia of the Bible, ed. by Pat Alexander
- The Macmillan Bible Atlas, by Aharoni and Avi-Yonah

COMMENTARIES (Read with discernment, compare at least three on any passage)

- Gospel Advocate Series
    - (older, conservative, beginner level of study)
- Burton Coffman Commentaries
    - (conservative, beginner level of study)
- The Living Word Commentary Series
    - (O.T. incomplete, conservative, beginner, out of print)
- The Bible Speaks Today Series
    - (practical, not by brotherhood, beginner to intermediate study)
- Truth for Today Commentary Series
    - (incomplete, new, conservative, intermediate study)
- Homer Hailey Commentaries
    - (incomplete, conservative, intermediate study)
- Old Testament Survey Series by James Smith
    - (incomplete, Christian Church, intermediate study)
- Tyndale New and Old Testament Commentaries
    - (not by brotherhood, intermediate study)
- Expositors Bible Commentary Series
    - (not by brotherhood, intermediate study)
- College Press Series
    - (church of Christ/Christian Church, intermediate to advanced study)
- N.T. Commentary by Hendrickson/Kistemaker
    - (not by brotherhood, intermediate to advanced)
- Expositor's Bible Commentary Series
    - (not by brotherhood, intermediate to advanced)
- New International Commentary Series, Erdmann's
    - (incomplete, not by brotherhood, advanced)
- The Pillar New Testament Commentary Series
    - (incomplete, not by brotherhood, Advanced)
- Word Biblical Commentary Series
    - (incomplete, not by brotherhood, advanced study)
- Keil-Delitzsch Old Testament commentaries
    - (older, advanced study)
- One Volume Commentaries - Adam Clark, Matthew Henry
    - (very old, beginner to intermediate)
- Commentary on Acts, two of the best are by Wayne Jackson and J.W. McGarvey
- The IVP Bible Background Commentary
    - (N.T. by Keener; O.T. by Walton, Matthews, etc.).

WORD STUDY BOOKS

- Mounce's Expository Dictionary of Old and New Testament Words (English based)
- Linguistic Key to the Greek New Testament, Fritz Rienecker, Trans. by Cleon Rogers, Jr.
- Theological Dictionary of New Testament Words, ed. by Bromiley (Greek and English index)
- A Greek-English Lexicon of the New Testament, by Bauer, Arndt, Gingrich, Danker (Greek bsd)
- A Greek-English Lexicon of the New Testament, Thayer (Greek based)
- New International Dictionary of New Testament Theology, ed. by Colin Brown
- Robertson's Word Pictures of the New Testament.
- Webster's English Dictionary

INTRODUCTIONS/BACKGROUNDS

- A Survey of Old Testament Introduction by Gleason Archer
- A Survey of the Old Testament by Andrew Hill and John Walton
- Old Testament Theology by Paul R. House
- The Old Testament Explorer by Charles Dyer and Gene Merrill
- New Testament Introduction by Donald Guthrie
- Introduction to the New Testament by Everett Harrison
- Survey of the New Testament by Robert Gundry
- Backgrounds of Early Christianity by Everett Fergeson
- New Testament History by F.F. Bruce
- New Testament Era by Bo Reick
- New Testament Times by Merrill Tenney.
- Manners and Customs of the Bible, by James M. Freeman
- The New Testament Background: Selected Documents, ed. by C.K. Barrett
- The Works of Josephus

PREACHING BOOKS

- Sermon Design and Delivery, 2nd edition, by Thomas H. Holland
- Encouraging Expository Preaching, 2nd edition, by Thomas H. Holland
- The Work of the Preacher is Working by Thomas H. Holland
- Man of God, edited by Shawn Mathis
- Reaching for Passion, edited by Dyer, Haynes, and Jenkins

• Speaking for the Master by Batsell Barrett Baxter (reprint by Hester Publ., Henderson, TN)
• Steps to the Sermon, by Brown, Clinard, and Northcutt (not church of Christ)
• Biblical Preaching, Haddon W. Robinson (not church of Christ)
• On the Preparation and Delivery of sermons, John A. Broadus, Rev. by Stanfield (not c of c)
• Between Two Worlds, by John R.W. Stott (not church of Christ)
• Reading Scripture in Public, Thomas Edward McComiskey (not church of Christ)
• Speaking to Teenagers by Fields and Robbins (not church of Christ)

YOUTH AND FAMILY MINISTRY

• The Youth Minister's Honeymoon by Enoch Rinks and Josh Hardin
• Your First Two Years in Youth Ministry by Doug Fields (not church of Christ)
• Purpose Driven Youth Ministry by Doug Fields (not church of Christ)
• Hurt 2.0: Inside the World of Today's Teenagers by Chap Clark (not church of Christ)
• Youth Culture 101 by Walt Mueller (not church of Christ)
• Family-Based Youth Ministry by Mark Devries (2004 edition, not church of Christ)
• Partnering with Parents by Burns and Devries (not church of Christ)
• Youth Ministry Nuts and Bolts by Duffy Robbins (revised edition, not church of Christ)
• Simple Youth Ministry
• Soul Searching by Smith and Denton (not church of Christ, cf. Transforming Student Ministry)
• Sticky Faith by Powell, Griffin, and Crawford (not church of Christ)
• Counseling Teenagers by Clinton and Clark (not church of Christ)

BIBLE LANGUAGE STUDIES
• Basics of Biblical Greek, William D. Mounce (textbook, workbook)
• Greek Grammar Beyond the Basics by Daniel B. Wallace
• A Practical Grammar for Classical Hebrew, J. Weingreen

MISCELLANEOUS BOOKS
• Roget's Thesaurus
• How We Got The Bible, by Neil R. Lightfoot
• The Journey from Texts to Translations by Wegner (not church of Christ)
• The English Bible from KJV to NIV by Jack Lewis

• Evidences: Convicted by Harrob, Focus Pr.; Behold, the Lamb of God, by Butt, Apologetics Pr.)
• All the Men of the Bible, All the Women of the Bible by Herbert Lockyer (not church of Christ)
• The Family of God by Batsell Baxter
• How to Study the New Testament Effectively by Guy N. Woods
• How to Read the Bible for All It's Worth by Fee and Stuart (not church of Christ)
• Walking With Those Who Weep by Ron and Don Williams
• Growing Through Grief by Bill Flatt
• The Search for the Ancient Order series by Earl West (Restoration history)
• The Seven Habits of Highly Effective People by Stephen R. Covey (non-religious)
• Handbook of Denominations by Mead and Hill (not church of Christ)
• The Leadership Challenge by Kouzes and Posner (non-religious book on leadership)

EVANGELISM/MISSIONS

• Missions: Rekindling the Fire by Turner and Shepherd
• Evangelism Made Simple by Stephen Rogers
• Fishers of Men Evangelism Training Series
• Connections Video for teens by Phillips and Montague, Focus Press
• Search for Truth DVD and book, John Moore, World Video Bible School
• Open Bible Study Tracts
• We Care Ministries Bible (checkbook edition)

SOFTWARE

• Accordance for Mac
• PC Study Bible (PC only)
• Logos Library System
• E-Sword

APPS

• Olive Tree Bibles
• ESV Study Bible for Olive Tree
• Glo Bible
• YouVersion Bibles

*I am grateful for the input of Wendell Robinson, Rusty Pettus, and Nick Jones.

SECTION FOUR
THE PRESS BOX

Just as there are announcers and reporters in the press box of the average ballpark, there are announcement leaders and scripture readers in the worship services of the church. I do not make this analogy to degrade the importance of worship, but merely as a memory tool. There are fewer and fewer men in our congregations. There are even fewer men who are willing to lead. We are in great need of men who will step forward and lead our congregations in worship to God.

Many who sign up to lead in public worship pay little attention to when it is their assigned turn to participate. Others do not take the time to call anyone if they cannot be present on their day to serve. If they do call someone, it is often at the last minute. Others take no time to prepare. Worship to God is not something to be thrown together at the last minute. It is not something to be taken lightly. It is one of the greatest privileges we will have in our lives. We must give it our reverence and our best effort.

This section is designed to help us to do that. I drew largely from Stafford North's *Church Leadership Training* as well as Jack Exum and Jim Strother's *Let's Have a Timothy Class.* I am grateful to all the congregations which took time to teach me to be a leader in worship.

SPEAKING DRILLS
(Stafford North)

**Emphasize underlined words and pause at /.

1.   Every member of the church/ <u>must be a worker.</u>

2.   <u>Prayer</u> can change your life.
      Prayer <u>can</u> change your life.
      Prayer can <u>change</u> your life.
      Prayer can change <u>your</u> life.
      Prayer can change your <u>life.</u>

3.   I believe that <u>Jesus Christ</u>/ is the <u>Son of God</u>.
      I believe that Jesus Christ <u>is</u>/ the Son of God.

4.   I am going to be a better Christian. Will <u>you</u>?

5. <u>Today</u>/ is the day of salvation.

6. He that <u>believes</u> and is <u>baptized</u>/ shall be <u>saved.</u>

7. So then <u>faith</u> comes by <u>hearing</u>/ and <u>hearing</u>/ by the <u>Word</u> of <u>God</u>.

MAKING ANNOUNCEMENTS

The announcements are not an act of worship. Yet, they are important. Many will not read the bulletin or written announcements. If we do not do the announcements vocally, they will be unaware of many activities. How well we do the announcements will have an impact on how involved the members will be.

I. **Purpose.**

    A.   EDIFY the congregation.

    B.   INFORM the congregation.
        1.   Fellowship activities.
        2.   Service opportunities.
        3.   Area meetings and workshops.
        4.   Illness and death in the congregation.

    C.   ENCOURAGE the members to be active and involved.

    D.   EXTEND a welcome at the beginning of service (some congregations separate this from the announcements).
        1.   Welcome visitors.
        2.   Remind members and visitors to fill out attendance cards.
        3.   Announce those leading in worship.
        4.   Prepare the audience for worship.
        5.   May also need to introduce the speaker (get info ahead of time).

    E.   EXIT: We may be called on to conclude services.
        1.   Announce the closing song and prayer.
        2.   Tell when the next service is.
        3.   Your may need to tell where the Lord's supper is served (Sunday night).

II. **Preparation.**

    A.   PRACTICE: Read over the announcements beforehand.

    B.   PICK: Announce only the necessary items (focus on the next week's activities).

    C.   PREPARE: Try to get additional announcements ahead of time.
        1.   Don't ask, "Are there other announcements?" You should already know.
        2.   You may have cards available for people to write down announcements.

3. Good to have a brief meeting of worship leaders just prior to worship.
    D. PAPER: Have the facts for each announcement written down (key word first).
    E. PRONOUNCE: Make sure you can pronounce all names and words.
    F. PLAN: Organize the announcements.
    G. PROPER dress (at least a tie, prefer a coat as well).

III. **Presentation.**
    A. STAND STRAIGHT and tall.
    B. START on time. Be punctual (at podium and ready to start on time).
    C. SPEAK loudly.
    D. SAY your words correctly. Pronounce and articulate properly.
    E. SPEED: Keep a good pace (not so slow they are bored, or so fast they can't follow).
    F. SINCERITY: Be dignified, friendly and sincere.
    G. SHOW the necessary emotions (sympathy for death, excitement for activity).
    H. STRESS the key facts of each announcement (emphasize key words and details).
    I. SAME: Vary your presentation (don't use the same phrases for welcoming etc.).
    J. SEE: Maintain good eye contact.
    K. SKIP nervous mannerisms (pacing, jingling keys etc.).

Conclusion

The sincerity, friendliness, or excitement we portray can have a big impact on the tone of the worship and on people's willingness to be involved.

Teacher Comments

Note: Give your book to your teacher when you make your class presentation.

Did the student...

1.	Dress PROPERLY? Was the student's appearance neat?	yes	no
2.	STAND STRAIGHT and tall?	yes	no
3.	SPEAK loudly?	yes	no
4.	SAY his words correctly? Pronounce and articulate properly?	yes	no
5.	Have proper SPEED? Did he keep a good pace?	yes	no
6.	Display SINCERITY? Was he dignified, friendly and sincere?	yes	no
7.	SHOW the necessary emotions?	yes	no
8.	STRESS the key facts of each announcement?	yes	no
9.	SEE? Maintain eye contact?	yes	no
10.	SKIP nervous mannerisms?	yes	no

COMMENTS:

SCRIPTURE READING

Intro: Scripture reading was an important part of the Synagogue worship in the first century (Lk. 4.16-20) and the services of the early Church (Col. 4.16). The Bible is the inspired Word of God (2 Tm. 3.15-17). Yet, it has taken a back seat in many of our worship assemblies. Let us return it to its rightful place.

I.   **Purpose** (not all inclusive).
   A.   To ALLOW God to speak through his Word (Ps. 119.105).
   B.   To PREPARE people's minds for worship.
   C.   To INTRODUCE the text of the sermon.

II.   **Preparation.**
   A.   PICK the passage.
      1.   Consider the audience (age etc.) and the occasion (theme etc.).
      2.   Ask the preacher if he has a text for his sermon.
      3.   It may be listed in the bulletin.
      4.   Make sure it conveys a complete thought.
   B.   PERCEIVE the basics of the passage.
      1.   Who is the author and audience?
      2.   What is the general story surrounding the passage?
      3.   What is the meaning and pronunciation of each word in the passage?
      4.   What kind of passage is it (proverb, parable, story, letter etc.)?
   C.   PRACTICE your delivery. Read it over several times (silently and out loud).
   D.   PAPER CLIP or book mark your text (keep small).
   E.   PUT on appropriate clothing which displays respect for the Word.

II.   **Presentation.**
   A.   SHARE: Announce the scripture and give the audience time to turn to it.
   B.   STAND STRAIGHT and tall as you read (firmly planted on both feet).
   C.   SPEAK LOUDLY so people can hear you (don't mumble).
   D.   SPEAK CLEARLY (pronounce words distinctly, make sure you voice "t" & "g" at the end of words).
   E.   SPEAK WITH PACE (not so slow it is boring or so fast they cannot follow).
   F.   SHOWMANSHIP: Bring the passage to life.
      1.   Bring the emotions of the passage out in your voice (mood changes).

2.   Reflect the question marks and exclamation points with your voice.
3.   Use your voice and a slight turn of your head to reflect character changes.
4.   Emphasize key words as you read the passage.
5.   Read in phrases or word groups instead of single words.

G.   SIGNS: Observe road signs such as "therefore," commas, periods etc. (pause).

H.   SEE: Maintain eye contact.
1.   <u>Pick up your Bible</u> when you read (not in front of your face).
2.   Use your finger to keep up with your location in the text.
3.   Read ahead (practice catching words at a glance, so you can look up).

Conclusion

God wanted the Bible to be read in public (Josh. 8; Neh. 8; Col. 4.16). Let us make sure that we prepare and present the Word in such a way that God is glorified.

Imagine that you are the only one in the world who has a Bible and you are in charge of reading it so people can understand it. How would you feel and what would you do? Remember that if you read the Bible in worship, it may be the only Bible that some of those people hear all week.

Teacher Comments

NOTE: Give your book to the teacher during class presentation.

Did the student...

1.   Dress neatly?   yes   no

2.   SHARE the scripture and give the audience time to turn to it?   yes   no

3.   STAND STRAIGHT and tall?   yes   no

4.   SPEAK LOUDLY?   yes   no

5.   SPEAK CLEARLY?   yes   no

6.   SPEAK WITH PACE?   yes   no

7.   Have SHOWMANSHIP? Bring the passage to life?   yes   no

8.   Observe SIGNS such as "therefore," commas, and periods? yes   no

9.   SEE? Maintain eye contact?   yes   no

10. Pick up his Bible?   yes   no

COMMENTS:

LEADING PRAYER

"The effective prayer of a righteous man can accomplish much. . . ." (James 5.16-18 NAS). In light of the power of prayer, it is an awesome responsibility to lead God's people before his throne.

I. **Purpose.**
   A. LEAD God's people in approaching his throne.
   B. EXPRESS gratitude.
   C. ASK for help.
   D. DECLARE God's greatness.

II. **Preparation.**
   A. Our HEARTS must be prepared.
      1. Do we believe (James 1.6-8)?
      2. Do we have a proper motive (James 4.3; Matt. 6.5-7)?
   B. Our HANDS must be prepared (1 Tim. 2.8). Are we right with God?
      1. Do we have any unrepented sin?
      2. Do we need to seek the forgiveness of a brother (Matt. 5.21-25)?
      3. Do we need to forgive another (Matt. 6.14-15)?
   C. Our BODIES must to be prepared (dress so as to show reverence).
   D. Our MINDS must to be prepared.
      1. Think about what you want to say.
      2. You may want to write down your thoughts.
      3. Note those who are ill or have lost loved ones.
      4. Think about current events that need to be prayed for (shooting, war etc.).
      5. Think about the occasion (mother's day, father's day etc).

III. **Presentation.**
   A. How to PRAY.
      1. PRONOUNCE and PACE: Pronounce words properly and pace your prayer such that is neither too fast nor too slow.
      2. REVERENCE and RESPECT God (may want to kneel when you pray).
      3. AVOID:
         a. PREACHING and PRIVATE PRAYERS.
            1) Don't preach. If you want to preach, ask the elders to do the lesson. Prayers are aimed primarily at God.

         2)   Don't pray a personal prayer (pray what applies to the congregation).

    b.   EMPLOYING big words to impress.

    c.   WELL-WORN sayings ("for whom it is our duty to pray," "ready recollection" etc.). Speak from your heart.

    d.   SAYING lengthy prayers and using vain repetition (Matt. 6.7).

  4.   YELL: Don't actually yell, but speak loudly so you can be heard.

B.   What to say? A good example is Matt. 6.9-13:
"Our Father who art in heaven, Hallowed be Thy name.'Thy kingdom come. Thy will be done, On earth as it is in heaven. Give us this day our daily bread. And forgive us our debts, as we also have forgiven our debtors. And do not lead us into temptation, but deliver us from evil" (NAS).

1.	Address God	"Our Father . . . "
2.	Praise God	"Hallowed be thy . . ."
3.	Pray for works of the church	"Thy kingdom . . ."
4.	Pray that God's will be done	"Thy will . . ."
5.	Ask for help with daily needs	"Give us . . . bread."
6.	Ask for forgiveness	"Forgive our debts."
7.	Ask for help in fighting temptation	"Deliver us from . . ."
8.	Pray in the name of Christ	(John 14.13-14)
9.	Conclude with "amen"	(1 Cor. 14.16; Rom. 16.24)

Conclusion

It is a tremendous privilege to be able to talk to God. We can all think of important people that we are unable to talk to. Yet, we have the opportunity daily to speak to the creator of the universe. Let us make sure we take it very seriously.

Teacher's Comments

NOTE: Give your book to the teacher when you make your class presentation.

Did the student...

1.	Dress neatly?	yes	no
2.	PRONOUNCE words properly?	yes	no
3.	PACE his prayer?	yes	no
4.	Show REVERENCE and RESPECT?	yes	no

5.   AVOID:

a.	PREACHING?	yes	no
b.	PRIVATE PRAYER?	yes	no
c.	EMPLOYING big words to impress?	yes	no
d.	WELL-WORN sayings?	yes	no
e.	SAYING a lengthy prayer and using vain repetition?	yes	no

6.	YELL? Speak loudly so he can be heard?	yes	no

COMMENTS:

THE LORD'S SUPPER

The Lord's supper is one of the key reasons the early church gathered together on the first day of the week (Acts 20.7; 1 Cor. 11.20). Our job as communion leaders is to help people focus on the sacrifice of Jesus. Consider the purpose of the Lord's supper:

> *For I received from the Lord that which I also delivered to you, that the Lord Jesus in the night in which He was betrayed took bread; and when He had given thanks, He broke it, and said, "This is My body, which is for you; do this in remembrance of Me." In the same way {He took} the cup also, after supper, saying, "This cup is the new covenant in My blood; do this, as often as you drink {it,} in remembrance of Me." For as often as you eat this bread and drink the cup, you proclaim the Lord's death until He comes. Therefore whoever eats the bread or drinks the cup of the Lord in an unworthy manner, shall be guilty of the body and the blood of the Lord. But let a man examine himself, and so let him eat of the bread and drink of the cup. (1 Cor. 11.23-29 NAS)*

I.   **Purpose.**
   A.   Look BACK.
      1.   Remember the body and blood of Christ (11.24-25).
      2.   Remember that Christ has made a new covenant (11.25).
      3.   Proclaim the Lord's death (11.26).
   B.   Look FORWARD - "till he comes" (11.26).
   C.   Look WITHIN - "examine himself" (11.28).

II.   **Preparation.**
   A.   Prepare you HEART. Examine your life and relationship with others (11.27-29).
   B.   Prepare your MIND.
      1.   Think about the death of Christ.
      2.   Think of what you are going to say to focus people on the Cross.
      3.   Think of what you are going to say in your prayer.
   C.   Prepare your BODY. Dress appropriately (shows respect).
   D.   Prepare your ACTIONS. Make sure you know your job during the communion.
      1.   Which aisle do you get? Do you serve the nursery? etc.
      2.   Where and when do you sit or stand?

3.   Where do people put the cups (in the pews or back in the trays)?

4.   Will there be a meeting before services of those helping with the supper?

III.   Presentation.

A.   PRESENT a reverent demeanor.

B.   PROJECT loudly.

C.   PRONOUNCE and articulate.

D.   PROPER PACE is important.

E.   PLACE the audience at the cross (help them focus - vary routine).

      1.   Might read a Scripture.

      2.   Might read the words of a song.

      3.   Make brief comments to focus thought.

F.   PRAY for the emblems (bread, then fruit of the vine).

      1.   Give thanks for Christ's sacrifice.

      2.   Note what emblems represent (bread/body - grape juice/blood).

      3.   Ask God to help us examine ourselves.

      4.   Pray from the heart (avoid well-worn sayings - "a manner well pleasing").

      5.   Christ's body was not broken on the cross.

G.   PASS out the communion trays.

      1.   Avoid clanging the trays or lids together.

      2.   Work efficiently, but not so hurried it takes from dignity of the service.

      3.   Don't do anything to call attention to yourself.

      4.   Watch for those who might have been overlooked.

      5.   When passing out the emblems, you will usually pass to every other row.

H.   Collection PLATE. The giving is often done at this time for convenience sake.

      1.   Remind the audience that it is a command of God (1 Cor. 16.1-2).

      2.   Find out what you do with the money trays afterward and if you are to help count the money?

      3.   In your prayer give thanks for the blessings that God has given us. You might ask for God's guidance in helping the elders know how best to use the money given.

Conclusion: Many place the Lord's supper at the end of services and it becomes an afterthought. Everyone is thinking more about going home than about Jesus. It is important that you help the congregation stay focused on Christ and the cross.

LEADING SINGING

The Gallup Organization reported these were the top five religious songs for Americans:

  1.   Amazing Grace
  2.   How Great Thou Art
  3.   Rock of Ages
  4.   Battle Hymn of the Republic
  5.   The Old Rugged Cross

(Princeton Religious Research Center's PRRC Emerging Trends, 10/88. Leadership, Vol. 10, no. 2). Songs have inspire humanity for thousands of years. You can probably think of special songs you have enjoyed singing during your lifetime (Amazing Grace, Jesus Loves Me etc). To be able to lead God's people in praising his name is a great privilege. Not everyone is cut out for it. Yet, you will never know if you can until you try. This is a brief introduction to the art of leading singing in worship.

I.   **Purpose:** Songs reach up to God and out to man.
      A.   WORSHIP.
           1.   It is a command of God (Col. 3.16-17; Eph 5.19).
           2.   It also sets the tone for the rest of worship. It has often been said that "great singing makes a great sermon."
      B.   WISDOM.
           1.   We speak to one another when we sing (Eph 5.19). Singing inspires those around us (cf. Paul and Silas singing in prison in Acts 16).
           2.   We also instruct one another (Eph. 5.19). The words of the songs teach and correct.

II.   **Preparation.**
      A.   FORETHOUGHT - Consider the following when choosing songs:
           1.   Preacher - Tie your songs into the message. The Sunday morning song leader and I try to get together each Thursday morning to coordinate his songs with my message. Thus, you can have two messages (song/sermon).
           2.   Purpose of service - Is it a prayer service, instillation of elders etc.?
           3.   Placement - Consider where the song is in the worship service (call to worship, before a prayer, before Lord's supper etc.).
           4.   People - Consider who is in your audience.
                a.   Is your audience primarily made up of young people, senior

saints, middle-aged or is it a mixture?

      b.   Try to avoid leading a number of new songs during worship.

          1)   It is hard for people to concentrate on worship if they are having to concentrate on learning the song.

          2)   This is especially important on Sunday mornings when you have a lot of visitors.

          3)   Have a designated time/class/service to learn new songs.

   5.   Practice.

      a.   Don't pick out your songs at the last minute. Pick them out ahead of time so you can practice them.

      b.   Keep a quick reference lists of songs that you know well in the back of your song book that you can use when you are called on at the last minute (have songs for an entire worship service as well as songs you can lead while waiting for a baptism).

B.   FATHER - You are leading God's people before his throne to praise his name. Pray that you may do it in accordance with his will.

C.   FITTING ATTIRE.

   1.   Dress to fit the occasion (Sunday morning worship, youth camp etc.).

   2.   As a general rule you need to be dress as well or better than anyone there.

   3.   I recommend wearing a coat and tie when leading for Sunday morning or evening services, as well as for Wednesday night services.

   4.   You should definitely wear a coat and tie for the Sunday morning service and I recommend at least a tie for the other services.

   5.   Your attire shows the importance of the gathering and your attitude toward worshiping God in song.

D.   FINDING YOUR SONGS

   1.   List your songs on a small index card or piece of paper which can be placed inside your song book or your coat pocket.

   2.   Mark the location of your songs in your song book so that they can be easily found (pieces of paper, paper clips, stick-it notes etc. - make sure that they do not look cluttered).

   3.   Arrive at least 15 minutes early to services to collect your thoughts and get your notes in order. This also allows time to adjust to last minute changes. Those leading in worship will often meet before services.

III. Presentation.

    A.   PITCH.

        1.   Avoid starting the song too high or too low (can make it difficult for some parts to sing their notes). If you do, it is ok to stop and start over. You made need to lower the song one step to accommodate the congregation.

        2.   A Pitch pipe can be very helpful in getting the right pitch.
a. You can blow the first note to help you start. The notes on the lines and spaces are named starting at the bottom line as follows: e, f, g, a, b, c, d, e, f. To find out if you should sharpen or flatten a note, look beside the treble cleft (discussed below) and see if there is a sharp or flat on that line or space. You then blow that note on your pitch pipe.

            b.   You can also blow the "do" note for the key it is in and each part can then find their note from the "do" note. Just remember that the "do" note for the key the song is in may not be the same note that the song actually starts with. The <u>song will start with either do, me, or so</u> of the key it is in.

            c.   There are eight notes in a major scale (a key). The notes are given letters as names: a, b, c, d, e, f, g. They move up from the "Do" note in the following pattern: Whole step, whole step, half step, whole step, whole step, whole step, half step. Sometimes sharps (raise the note a half step) and flats (lower the note a half step) will be added to make these steps possible. These steps are called: do, re, me, fa, so, la, ti, do.

            d.   The example below is the Key of "C." The base note, or "do" is the "C" note. Thus you would blow the letter "C" on your pitch pipe if the song was in the key of "C." Again, remember that this note may not necessarily be the note that the song starts on.

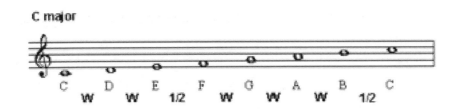

C major

You can learn what key a song is in by looking at what is next to the treble cleft (discussed below) (cf. Jackson 21).

C major

The key of "C" has no sharp or flat signs at the beginning of the song (memorize this).

F major

The key of "F" has one flat at the beginning of the song (memorize this).

D major

If there are sharps at the beginning of a song, find the next line or space above the last sharp (reading from left to right) and that line or space is the key.

Bb major

If there are flats at the beginning of the song, find the next to last flat (from left to right) and that is the key of the song.

B.   PACE.
1.   Do not lead every song at the same speed. Pay attention to the musical notations which give directions on how fast or slow to sing the song. Do not get into a rut.
2.   A song does not have to be sung at the speed of light to express excitement or joy and it does not have to be sung at the speed of drying paint just to express meaning or sincerity.

3. Hand motions can help the audience to stay together at the same pace.
    The following are the common hand motions for keeping time:

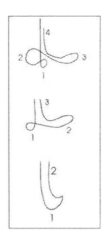

4. Use your hand to signal which verse you will sing next.
    a. Raise your hand and show the number of the next verse during the last line of the verse you are on and leave it up during the first line of the next verse.
    b. Use a closed fist to signify the 6th verse.
5. Use a motion of your choosing to show the audience when to stop singing.

C. POWER.
    1. Sing with feeling. Express the emotions of the song in your voice (yet, remember you are not an entertainer).
    2. If you are not excited about singing, then they will not be.
    3. "When placed in command, take charge" (Gen. Norman Schwartskopf). You are the leader, so lead. Do not let the congregation lead you. This can also aid keeping pace (the audience will keep pace with a strong voice).
    4. Start strong so they will be compelled to join you. If you are timid or unsure in starting the song the congregation will be timid in their singing, or some in the audience will try to lead it for you and create confusion.
    5. Encourage your audience to keep their eyes on you. Keep your eyes on them to get feedback (Are they struggling to hear, lagging

behind etc?).

D. PRESENT THE SONG.
1. Announce the song number (not page number) in a loud and distinct manner (don't mumble).
2. I usually announce the number, say each number separately, and then announce it again (i.e., "four hundred and twelve; that's four, one, two; four hundred and twelve).
3. Tell them which verses you plan to sing.
4. Don't preach before the song or keep your comments short.
5. Don't apologize for a soar throat, if possible, before you sing or at least mention it as little as possible (they will focus more on your throat than singing the song).
6. You do not have to sing every verse of every song. Be conscious of time. You may need to adjust during the service (i.e., after an exceptionally long prayer). Allow the preacher plenty of time for his message.
6. Never stop singing while people are still responding to the invitation (others will think they cannot respond).
7. Start singing the invitation song immediately after the last word of the sermon. A lull between the sermon and the song can destroy the effectiveness of the invitation. Be aware that the preacher may want to stop the song to make a comment (do not stop the song to make comments yourself, let the preacher handle it).

Conclusion

You do not have to sing perfectly to sing praises to God. Yet, if we are going to lead God's people in praising his name, we want to do our very best (special thanks to Jerry Elder for his input in developing this section).

BASIC MUSIC THEORY

Music is written on what is called a **staff**, which consists of 5 lines and the 4 spaces between those lines.

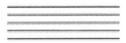

Music is often written in a **treble clef**. Treble clef is also referred to as the G clef with the center of the clef circling the G note on the 2nd line up.

Music is divided into sections called **measures** by vertical lines called **bar lines**.

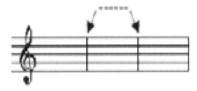

At the end of a song is a **final double bar line** which indicates the end of the piece.

A **repeat sign** is used to play a section of music again (Looks the same as a final double bar line only with 2 dots).

Here is a little saying to remember the names of the notes on the treble staff (theory and graphics from www.cyberfret.com).

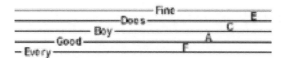

APPENDIX A
WHAT IS PREACHING?

*"Preaching is the **investigation, translation, organization, illustration,** and **application** of **Inspiration** with the goal of **transformation** in the lives of those who need **justification** and **sanctification**"* (WKB, 9-13-06, edited 2013). Preaching is making sure that the inspired message of the 1st century is understood and lived out in the 21st century.

Investigation: Draw out the original meaning of Scripture by diligent study.

Translation: Put the original meaning into contemporary words/thoughts.

Organization: Organize your research so it is accessible to yourself & others.

Illustration: Inspire people to understand, remember, and act on the text.

Application: Help people know how they should think/live differently.

Transformation: Preaching should guide and motivate people to accept Christ (justification/salvation) and live like Christ (sanctification). This will require radical change (transformation).

Justification: This is the moment of conversion/salvation. God is declaring us to be just or righteous in spite of our sins based on faith in Christ that is expressed in repentance, confession, and baptism.

Sanctification: This is the ongoing process of transformation into the likeness of Christ that takes place after conversion (justification).

*According to research done in 2010, about 30% of the Bible majors at church of Christ schools want to be preachers (Brothers, *A Cross-Cultural Study…*, 2010). May you be one of the 30%!

1 Tim 4:6-16 *6 If you <u>instruct</u> the brethren in these things, you will be a **good minister of Jesus Christ**, <u>nourished</u> in the words of faith and of the good doctrine which you have carefully followed. 7 But <u>reject</u> profane and old wives' fables, and <u>exercise</u> yourself toward godliness. 8 For bodily exercise profits a little, but godliness is profitable for all things, having promise of the life that now is and of that which is to come. 9 This is a faithful saying and worthy of all acceptance. 10 For to this end we both <u>labor and suffer reproach</u>, because we trust in the living God, who is the Savior of all men, especially of those who believe. 11 These things <u>command and teach</u>. 12 <u>Let no one despise</u> your youth, but <u>be an example</u> to the believers in word, in conduct, in love, in spirit, in faith, in purity. 13 Till I come, <u>give attention to reading, to exhortation, to doctrine</u>. 14 <u>Do not neglect the gift</u> that is in you, which was given to you by* *prophecy with the laying on of the hands of the eldership. 15 <u>Meditate</u> on these things; <u>give yourself entirely</u> to them, that your progress may be evident to all. 16 <u>Take heed</u> to yourself and to the doctrine. <u>Continue</u> in them, for in doing this you <u>will save</u> both yourself and those who hear you. NKJV*

THE GOOD MINISTER OF JESUS CHRIST (1 Tim. 4:6-16)

Nutrition - Feed on the Word (4:6, 13)
Illustration - Live out the Word (4:7-8, 12, 15-16)
Instruction - Teach the Word (4:6, 11, 13-16)
Motivation - Exhort obedience to the Word (4:11, 13, 16)
Persecution - Suffer for the Word (4:10)

WORKS CITED

Baxter, Richard. *The Reformed Pastor*. Ed. by James M. Houston. Reprinted. Classics of Faith and Devotion. Dallas: Multnomah Books, 1982.

Beatty, Chris. *The Vocal Coach: Speakers*. Video. Franklin: Ministry Music, 1990.

Blair, Brett., ad. 2006. *Sermon Illustrations.com*. Retrieved 5 September 2006 from www.sermonillustrations.com/a-z/b/bible_ignorance_of.htm. 2006.

Broadus, John A. *On the Preparation and Delivery of Sermons*. 1870. 4th ed. Rev. by Vernon L. Stanfield. San Francisco: Harper, 1979.

Brooks, Phillips. *Lectures on Preaching*. New York: E. P. Dutton , 1907.

Brothers, Kirk. 2010. A Cross-Cultural Study of Factors Motivating church of Christ Ministry Students to Enter Ministry. Dissertation submitted at The Southern Baptist Theological Seminary.

Brown, H.C. Jr., H. Gordon Clinard, and Jesse J. Northcutt. *Steps to the Sermon*. Nashville: Broadman, 1963.

Carnegie, Dale. *Public Speaking and Influencing Men in Business*. 1926. 47th printing. New York: Association Press, 1953.

___. *The Quick and Easy Way to Effective Speaking*. 1962. Rev. by Dorothy Carnegie. 25th printing. Garden City: Dale Carnegie and Associates, 1982.

Draper, Edyth. *Biblical Illustrator*. Version 3.0e. CD ROM. Parsons Technology, 1998.

Exum, Jack and Jim Strother. *Let's Have a Timothy Class*. Exum Publications 1973.

Elder, Jerry. Youth Minister. West 7th Street church of Christ. Telephone interview. May 2002.

Farrar, Steve. *The Point Man*. Dallas: Multnomah Books, 1990.

Fee, Gordon D. and Douglas Stuart. *How to Read the Bible for All Its Worth*. 1982. Grand Rapids: Academie, 1991.

Guild, Claude A. *Training Men to Preach*. Springfield: Guild Publications, 1968.

Hall, Jess Jr. "Preaching - Illustrating the Sermon." <u>Firm Foundation</u>. 21February 2001. <u>http://www.bible-infonet.org/ff/articles/preaching/112_11_01.htm</u>.

___. "Where Should Illustrations Be Used in the Sermon." <u>Firm Foundation</u>. Accessed 21 February 2001. <u>http://www.bible-infonet.org/ff/articles/preaching/</u> <u>112_11_01.htm</u>.

Holland, Thomas H. *Encouraging Expository Preaching*. 1981. 2nd edition. Brentwood: Penmann, 2000.

___. *Sermon Design and Delivery*. 1967. 2nd edition 1995. 10th printing. Brentwood: Penmann, 2000.

Holy Bible: New King James Version. *PC Study Bible*. Version 4.2b. CD Rom. Seatle: BibleSoft, 2004.

Holy Bible: Updated New American Standard Bible. *PC Study Bible*. Version 4.2B. CD Rom. Seattle: BibleSoft, 2004.

International Standard Bible Encyclopedia. PC Study Bible. Version 3.2e. CD Rom. Seatle: BibleSoft, 2001.

Jackson, James L. *Church Music Handbook*. Nashville: David Lipscomb, 1983.

Jamieson, Fausset, and Brown Commentary. PC Study Bible. Version 4.2B. CD Rom. Seatle: BibleSoft, 2004.

Johnston, Jeff. Youth Minister. Ethridge church of Christ. Telephone interview. May 2002.

Kougle, Kathleen. *Primer for Public Speaking*. New York: Harper and Row, 1988.

Kruger, Arthur N. *Effective Speaking: A Complete Course*. New York: Van Nostrand Reinhold, 1970.

Larkin, Marilynn. "Sleep on it." *FINDARTICLES.COM*. 28 November 2000. <<u>http://www.findarticles.com.</u>>.

Lightfood, Neil R. *The Parables of Jesus: Part 1*. The Living Word. Austin: Sweet, 1963.

Lockyer, Herbert. *All the Men of the Bible*. 1958. Grand Rapids: Zondervan, 1982.

___. *All the Parables of the Bible*. 1963. Grand Rapids: Zondervan, 1995.

Loyd, Dennis. Retired Literature professor from David Lipscomb University and elder at the Granny White Church of Christ, Nashville. Telephone interview. April 2001.

McComiskey, Thomas Edward. *Reading Scripture in Public*. Grand Rapids: Baker, 1991.

Mathis, Shawn, ed. *Man of God*. Nashville; Gospel Advocate, 1996.

North, Stafford. *Church Leadership Training*. Oklahoma City: Oklahoma Christian, 1969.

___. "Hermeneutics 101." *Gospel Advocate*. May 96.

Polhill, John. Toward a biblical view of call. In *Preparing for Christian ministry: An evangelical approach*. ed. David P. Gushee and Walter C. Jackson. Wheaton, Illinois; Victor Books, 1996. 65-79.

Robinson, Haddon W. *Biblical Preaching: The Development and Delivery of Expository Messages*. Grand Rapids: Baker, 1980.

Schmidt, K. L., III. *Theological Dictionary of the New Testament*. Gerhard Kittel and Gerhard Friedrich., eds. Abridged in one volume by Geoffrey W. Bromiley. Reprint. Grand Rapids: Eerdmans, 1985.

Smith, Billy R. "Advanced Preaching." Class lecture. Freed-Hardeman University. Henderson, TN. Spring 1996.

Stott, John R.W. *Between Two Worlds*. 1982. Reprinted. Grand Rapids: Eerdman's, 1983.

Schwartskopf, Norman. Speech delivered at Freed-Hardeman University. Henderson, TN. 7 Dec 2001.

Thayer's Greek Lexicon. PC Study Bible. Version 3.2e. CD Rom. Seatle: BibleSoft, 2001.

The Mac Attack: The Road to 62 and Beyond. Tulsa: Trade Life books, 1998.

Wigram, George. 2004. *The Englishman's Greek concordance, PC Study Bible*, Version 4.2B, CD ROM. Seattle: Biblesoft.

Willimon, William H. 2002. *Pastor: The theology and practice of ordained ministry*. Nashville: Abingdon Press.

Winkler, Dan. Pulpit Minister. Huntington church of Christ. Telephone interview. April 2001.

Woods, Guy N. *How to Study the New Testament Effectively*. Nashville: Gospel Advocate, 1992.

Bibliography of Available Works on Preaching/Speaking

**I have not read and do not personally endorse all of these works. They are included in this book in case readers (especially college students or those who might teach this book) want to do additional study of homiletics (the art and craft of preaching) on their own.

Abbey, Merrill R. 1963. *Preaching to the contemporary mind.* Nashville: Abingdon.

_____. 1973. *Communication in pulpit and parish.* Philadelphia: Westminster.

Achtemeir, Elizabeth. 1973. *The Old Testament and the proclamation of the Gospel.* Philadelphia: Westminster.

_____. 1980. *Creative preaching.* Nashville: Abingdon.

_____. 1987. *Preaching about family relationships.* Philadelphia: Westminster.

Adams, Jay E. 1982. *Preaching with purpose: The urgent task of homiletics.* Grand Rapids: Zondervan.

_____. 1983. *Essays on biblical preaching.* Grand Rapids: Zondervan.

Allen, Bob. 2005. *Sermon CPR.* Kansas City: Beacon Hill Press.

Allen, Ronald J. 1992. *Preaching the topical sermon.* Louisville: Westminster/John Knox Press.

Armstrong, James. 1977. *Telling truth: the foolishness of preaching in a real world.* Waco: Word Books.

Beatty, Chris. 1990. *The vocal coach: Speakers.* Video. Franklin: Ministry Music.

Broadus, John A. 1979. *On the preparation and delivery of sermons.* 4th ed. Rev. by Vernon L. Stanfield. San Francisco: Harper.

Brooks, Phillips. 1907. *Lectures on preaching.* New York: E. P. Dutton.

Brown, H. C., Gordon H. Clinard, Jesse J. Northcutt, and Al Fasol. 1996. *Steps to the sermon.* Nashville: Broadman & Holman.

Bailey, Raymond. 1991. *Paul the preacher.* Nashville: Broadman.

_____. 1990. *Jesus the preacher.* Nashville: Broadman.

Barclay, William. 1966. *Fishers of men.* Philadelphia: Westminster.

Bartlett, David. 1983. *The shape of Scriptural authority.* Philadelphia: Fortress Press.

Bartlett, Gene E. 1962. *The audacity of preaching.* New York: Harper and Brothers.

Bartow, Charles. 1980. *The preaching moment.* Nashville: Abingdon.

Bauman, J. Daniel. 1972. *An introduction to contemporary preaching.* Grand Rapids: Baker Book House.

Baxter, Batsell Barrett. 1971. *Heart of the Yale lectures.* Grand Rapids: Baker.

_____. 1999. *Speaking for the master.* Reprint. Henderson, TN: Hester Publications.

Baxter, Richard. 1982. *The reformed pastor.* Ed. by James M. Houston. Reprinted. Classics of Faith and Devotion. Dallas: Multnomah Books.

Berkley, James D., ed. 1986. *Preaching to convince.* Wheaton: Christianity Today Press.

Best, Ernest. 1978. *From Text to sermon: Responsible use of the New Testament in preaching.* Atlanta: John Knox Press.

Blackwood, Andrew W. 1941. *Preaching from the Bible.* Nashville: Abingdon.

_____. 1942. *Planning a year's pulpit work.* Nashville: Abingdon.

_____. 1942. *The Funeral.* Philadelphia: Westminster.

_____. 1948. *The preparation of sermons.* Nashville: Abingdon.

Bodey, Richard Allen, ed. 1990. *Inside the sermon: Thirteen preachers discuss their methods of preparing messages.* Grand Rapids: Baker.

Brooks, Phillips. 1969. *Lectures on preaching.* Reprint of 1877 Lyman Beecher (Yale)

Lectures. Grand Rapids: Baker.

Browne, Benjamin. 1977. *Illustrations for preaching*. Nashville: Broadman.

Brown, Robert. 1976. *The ministry of the Word*. Philadelphia: Fortress.

Bryson, Harold T. and James C. Taylor. 1980. *Building sermons to meet people's needs*. Nashville: Broadman.

_____. 1995. *Expository preaching: The art of preaching through a book of the Bible*. Nashville: Broadman & Holman.

Buerlein, Homer K. 1986. *How to preach more powerful sermons*. Philadelphia: Westminster.

Buttrick, David. 1987. *Homiletic moves and structures*. Philadelphia: Fortress. Baehr, Theodore. 1986. *Getting the Word out: How to communicate the Gospel in today's world*. San Francisco: Harper and Row.

Carnegie, Dale. 1953. *Public speaking and influencing men in business*. 47th printing. New York: Association Press.

_____. 1982. *The quick and easy way to effective speaking*. Rev. by Dorothy Carnegie. 25th printing. Garden City: Dale Carnagie and Associates.

Carter, Terry, J. Scott Duvall, and J. Daniel Hays. 2005. *Preaching God's Word*. Grand Rapids: Zondervan.

Carl, William J. 1984. *Preaching Christian doctrine*. Philadelphia: Fortress.

Casey, Michael W. 1995. *Saddlebags, city streets, and cyberspace: A history of preaching in the Churches of Christ*. Abilene: ACU Press.

Chartier, Myron. 1981. *Preaching as communication*. Nashville: Abingdon.

Chapell, Bryan. 2005. *Christ centered preaching*. 2nd ed. Grand Rapids: Baker Books.

Claypool, John. 1980. *The preaching event*. Waco: Word.

Cleland, James T. 1965. *Preaching to be understood*. New York: Abingdon.

Cox, James W. 1976. *A guide to Biblical preaching*. Nashville: Abingdon.

_____. ed. 1983. *Biblical preaching: An expositor's treasure*. Philadelphia: West minster.

_____. 1985. *Preaching*. San Francisco: Harper and Row.

Craddock, Fred B. 1978. *Overhearing the Gospel*. Lyman Beecher (Yale) Lectures. Nashville: Abingdon.

_____. 1979. *As one without authority*. Nashville: Abingdon.

_____. 1985. *Preaching*. Nashville: Abingdon.

Daane, James. 1980. *Preaching with confidence: A theological essay on the power of the pulpit*. Grand Rapids: Eerdmans.

Davis, H. Grady. 1958. *Design for preaching*. Philadelphia: Fortress.

Davis, Ken. 1991. *Secrets of dynamic communication: Preparing & delivering powerful speeches*. Grand Rapids: Zondervan.

Demaray, Donald E. 1990. *Introduction to homiletics*. Grand Rapids: Baker.

Dodd, C. H. 1936. *Apostolic preaching*. London: Hodder and Stoughton.

Duduit, Michael, Ed. 1992. *Handbook of contemporary preaching*. Nashville: Broadman.

Duke, Robert. 1980. *The sermon as God's Word: Theologies for preaching*. Nashville: Abingdon.

Dyer, Russell, Tommy Haynes, and Jeff Jenkins, eds. 2005. *Reaching for passion: The heart of preaching and the preachers heart*. Oklahoma City: Clarity Publications.

Edge, Findley B. 1999. *Teaching for results*. Rev. ed. Nashville: Broadman and Holman.

Edwards, J. Kent. 2005. *Effective first-person biblical preaching*. Grand Rapids: Zondervan.

Erdahl, Lowell O. 1976. *Preaching for the people*. Nashville: Abingdon.

Eslinger, Richard L. 1996. *Pitfalls in preaching*. Grand Rapids: Eerdmans.

Fant, Clyde E. 1975. *Preaching for today*. New York: Harper and Row.

Fant, Clyde and William M. Pinson, Jr. 1971. *Twenty centuries of Great preaching*. 12 Vol. Waco: Word.

Farmer, H. H. 1977. *The servant of the Word*. Reprint. Philadelphia: Fortress.

Faw, Chalmer E. 1962. *A guide to Biblical preaching*. Nashville: Broadman.

Fee, Gordon D. 1983. *New Testament exegesis*. Philadelphia: Westminster.

Fee, Gordon D., and Douglas Stuart. 1982. *How to read the Bible for all its worth*. Grand Rapids: Zondervan.

Filkins, Kenn. 1992. *Comfort those who mourn: How to preach personalized funeral messages*. Joplin, MO: College Press.

Fisher, David. 1996. *The 21st-century pastor*. Grand Rapids: Zondervan.

Forsyth, P. T. 1980. *Positive thinking and the modern mind*. Reprint of the 1907 Lyman Beecher (Yale) Lectures on Preaching. Grand Rapids: Baker.

Fuller, Reginald. 1980. *The use of the Bible in preaching*. Philadelphia: Fortress.

Gibson, George M. 1980. *Planned preaching*. Philadelphia: Westminster.

Gowan, Donald E. 1980. *Reclaiming the Old Testament for the Christian pulpit*. Atlanta: John Knox.

Greidanus, Sidney. 1988. *The modern preacher and the ancient Text: Interpreting and preaching Biblical literature*. Grand Rapids: Eerdmans.

Gresham, Charles and Keith Keeran. 1991. *Evangelistic preaching*. Joplin: College Press.

Hall, Thor. 1971. *The future shape of preaching*. Philadelphia: Fortress.

Halvorson, Arndt L. 1982. *Authentic preaching*. Minneapolis: Augsburg.

Hayes, John H. and Carl R. Holladay. 1982. Biblical exegesis: *A beginner's handbook*. Atlanta: John Knox.

Holland, DeWitte. 1969. *Preaching in American history*. Nashville: Abingdon.

_____. 1971. *Sermons in American history*. Nashville: Abingdon.

_____. 1980. The *preaching tradition: A brief history*. Nashville: Abingdon.

Holland, Thomas H. 2000. *Encouraging Expository Preaching*. 2nd ed. Brentwood: Penmann.

_____. 2000. *Sermon design and delivery*. 10th printing. Brentwood: Penmann.

____. 2001. *The work of the preacher is working*. Brentwood: Penmann.

Hostetler, Michael J. 1986. *Introducing the sermon: The art of compelling beginnings*. Grand Rapids: Zondervan.

Hughes, Robert. 1985. *A trumpet in darkness: Preaching to mourners*. Philadelphia: Fortress.

Hunt, Ernest E. 1982. *Sermon struggles: Four methods of sermon preparation*. New York: Seabury.

Hybels, Bill, and Stuart Briscoe, and Haddon Robinson. 1990. *Mastering contemporary preaching*. Portland: Multnomah.

Jackson, Edgar N. 1972. *How to preach to people's needs*. Reprint ed. Grand Rapids: Baker.

Kaiser, Walter C. 1973. *The Old Testament in contemporary preaching*. Grand Rapids: Baker.

Keck, Leander. 1978. *The Bible in the pulpit: The renewal of Biblical preaching*. Nashville: Abingdon.

Killinger, John. 1985. *Fundamentals of Preaching*. Philadelphia: Fortress.
Koller, Charles. 1997. *How to preach without notes*. Paperback ed. Grand Rapids: Baker.

Kougle, Kathleen. 1988. *Primer for public speaking*. New York: Harper and Row.

Kruger, Arthur N. 1970. *Effective speaking: A complete course*. New York: Van Nostrand Reinhold.

Larsen, David L. 1992. *Evangelism mandate: Recovering the centrality of Gospel preaching*. Wheaton: Crossway Books.

_____. 1995. *Telling the old, old story: The art of narrative preaching*. Wheaton: Crossway.

Leach, William H., ed. 1961. *The Cokesbury Marriage Manual*. Nashville: Abingdon.

Lewis, Ralph L. and Gregg Lewis. 1983. *Inductive preaching: Helping people listen*. Westchester: Crossway.

Linn, Edmund H. 1966. *Preaching as counseling*. Valley Forge: Judson Press.

Long, Thomas G. 1989. *Preaching and the literary forms of the Bible*. Philadelphia: Fortress Press.

_____. 2005. *The witness of preaching*. 2nd ed. Westminster: John Knox.

Lueking, F. Dean. 1985. *Preaching: The art of connecting God and people*. Waco: Word.

MacArthur, John. 2005. *Preaching: How to preach biblically*. Nashville: Thomas Nelson.

MacArthur, John F. and the Master's Seminary faculty. 1992. *Rediscovering expository preaching*. Dallas: Word.

_____. 1993. *Ashamed of the Gospel: When the church becomes like the world*. Wheaton: Crossway.

Marcel, Pierre C. 1963. *The prevalence of preaching*. Grand Rapids: Baker.

Massey, James Earl. 1974. *The responsible pulpit*. Anderson: Warner Press.

Mathis, Shawn, ed. 1996. *Man of God*. Nashville: Gospel Advocate.

McClure, John, et al. 2005. *Listening to listeners: Homiletical case studies*. Chalice Press.

McComiskey, Thomas Edward. 1991. *Reading Scripture in public*. Grand Rapids: Baker.

McDill, Wayne. 1994. *The twelve essential skills for great preaching*. Nashville: Broadman & Holman.

_____. 1999. *Moment of truth: A guide to effective sermon delivery*. Nashville: Broadman & Holman.

McLaughlin, Raymond W. 1979. *The ethics of persuasive preaching*. Grand Rapids: Baker.

Miller, Calvin. 1994. *The empowered communicator: 7 keys to unlocking an audience*. Nashville: Broadman.

_____. 1995. *The empowered leader: Ten keys to servant leadership*. Nashville: Broadman & Holman.

Miller, Donald G. 1957. *The way to biblical preaching: How to communicate the Gospel in Depth*. Nashville: Abingdon.

_____. 1976. *Fire in thy mouth*. Reprint ed. Grand Rapids: Baker.

Mounce, Robert H. 1962. *The essential nature of New Testament preaching*. Grand Rapids: Eerdmans.

Olford, Stephen F. 1998. *Anointed expository preaching*. Nashville: Broadman & Holman.

Pearce, J. Winston. 1967. *Planning your preaching*. Nashville: Broadman & Holman.

Peterson, Eugene H. and Miller, Calvin, compilers. 1987. *Weddings, funerals, and special events. The leadership library*. Vol. 10. Carol Stream, IL: Christianity Today.

Polhill, John. 1996. Toward a biblical view of call. In *Preparing for Christian ministry: An evangelical approach*. ed. David P. Gushee and Walter C. Jackson. Wheaton: Victor Books. 65-79.

Richard, Ramesh. 2005. *Preparing Evangelistic Sermons*. Grand Rapids: Baker.

Richards, Lawrence O. and Gary Bredfeldt. 1998. *Creative Bible teaching*. Rev. ed. Chicago: Moody Press.

Robinson, Haddon W. 1980. *Biblical preaching: The development and delivery of expository sermons*. Grand Rapids: Baker.

_____. ed. 1989. *Biblical sermons: How twelve preachers apply the principles of Biblical preaching*. Grand Rapids: Baker.

_____. 1999. *Making a difference in preaching*. Scott Gibson, ed. Grand Rapids: Baker.

Robinson, Haddon and Craig Brian Larson. 2005. *The art and craft of biblical preaching*. Grand Rapids: Zondervan.

Robinson, Haddon and Torrey Robinson. 2003. *It's all in how you tell it: Preaching first-person expository messages*. Grand Rapids: Baker.

Sleeth, Ronald E. 1986. *God's Word and our words*. Atlanta: John Knox.

Smart, James D. 1970. *The strange silence of the Bible in the Church*. Philadelphia: Westminster.

Smith, Billy R. 1990. Designing a program of planned preaching for the Estes Church of Christ: Henderson, TN. A Thesis. Henderson, TN.

Stauderman, Albert P. 1983. *Let me illustrate: Stories and quotations for Christian communicators*. Minneapolis: Augsburg.

Stevenson, Dwight E. 1956. *Preaching on the books of the New Testament*. New York: Harper and Brothers.

_____. 1961. *Preaching on the books of the Old Testament*. New York: Harper and Brothers.

Stewart, James S. 1946. *Heralds of God*. New York: Scribner's.

_____. 1953. *A faith to proclaim*. New York: Scribner's.

Stott, John R.W. 1983. *Between two worlds*. Reprint. Grand Rapids: Eerdman's.

Stuart, Douglas. 1980. *Old Testament exegesis*. Philadelphia: Westminster.

Switzer, David. 1979. *Pastor, preacher, person: Developing a pastoral ministry in depth*. Nashville: Abingdon.

Thompson, William D. 1981. *Preaching biblically: Exegesis and interpretation*. Nashville: Abingdon.

Wardlaw, Don M., ed. 1983. *Preaching biblically: Creating sermons in the shape of Scripture*. Philadelphia: Westminster.

Whitesell, Faris D. and Lloyd M. Perry. 1954. *Variety in your preaching*. Westwood: Revell.

Wiersbe, Warren W. and Lloyd M. Perry. 1984. *The Wycliffe handbook of preaching and preachers*. Chicago: Moody.

Wiersbe, Warren W. 1994. *Preaching & teaching with imagination: The quest for biblical ministry*. Wheaton: Victor Books.

Willimon, William H. 1992. *Peculiar speech: Preaching to the baptized*. Grand Rapids: Eerdmans.

_____. 1994. *Intrusive Word: Preaching to the unbaptized*. Grand Rapids: Eerdmans.

_____. 2002. *Pastor: The theology and practice of ordained ministry*. Nashville: Abingdon Press.

_____. 2005. *Proclamation and theology*. Nashville: Abingdon.

Wilson, Paul Scott. 1999. *The four pages of the sermon: A guide to biblical preaching*.

Nashville: Abingdon Press.

Wiseman, Neil B. 1977. *Biblical preaching for contemporary man*. Grand Rapids: Baker.

Wilson, Paul Scott. 2005. *Broken words: Reflections on the craft of preaching.* Nashville: Abingdon

Yount, William R. 1996. *Called to learn: A Christian teacher's introduction to educational psychology*. Nashville: Broadman & Holman.

_____. 1999. *Called to teach*. Nashville: Broadman and Holman.

PHOTO CREDITS

Coach giving signals (Clevland Indians) on page 32 courtesy of MarvinWilliams.org. http://cl.ly/OdX7

Picture of Jose Reyes (New York Mets) on page 47 courtesy of USA Today. http://cl.ly/OdRK

Picture of David Ortiz (Boston Red Sox) on page 58 courtesy of MLBsluggers.com. http://cl.ly/Odac

All other photos not cited are via a subscription to **ThinkStockPhotos.com**.

Made in the USA
Lexington, KY
09 February 2016